Pillars of the Hebrew Nation Part I

by

Tammy Duby

Featuring

Graphic Organizers

by

Dinah Zike

Common Sense Press

Pillars of History is a comprehensive project which is projected to include the titles below. Please check our website for updates and product availability.

Pillars of History:
> *Pillars of the Hebrew Nation, Part I*
> *Pillars of the Hebrew Nation, Part II*

Copyright © 2009 by:
> Common Sense Press
> 8786 Highway 21
> Melrose, FL 32666
> *www.commonsensepress.com*

> Dinah Zike
> www.dinah.com

Printed in the United States of America
ISBN 978-1-929683-27-7

The term "Pizza Book" is copyrighted by Tammy and Mike Duby of Tobin's Lab and used by permission. For more information visit Tobin's Lab on the world wide web.

The authors and the publisher have made every reasonable effort to ensure that the activities in this book are safe when performed according to the book's instructions. We assume no responsibility for any damage sustained or caused while performing the activities in Pillars of History. We further recommend that students undertake these activities under the supervision of a teacher, parent, and/or guardian.

Pillars of History, Part I

Table of Contents

Pillars of the Hebrew Nation, Part I

Overview

Part I

1. God Creates the World
2. The First People
3. Adam and Eve Disobey God
4. Cain and Abel
5. Noah Found Grace
6. Tower of Babel
7. Job
8. Abraham, Man of Faith
9. Isaac, Son of Promise
10. Jacob, Man of Two Names
11. Joseph the Dreamer
12. Joseph the Ruler
13. Birth of Moses
14. Moses the Deliverer
15. Pharoah Meets the One True God
16. Passover and the Red Sea
17. God's Care in the Desert
18. God Gives Ten Commandments
19. A Tabernacle for God
20. Twelve Spies
21. Rahab Saves Two Spies
22. Two Wicked Cities
23. Joshua is Tricked
24. The Sun Stands Still and Five Kings are Defeated

Pillars of History, Part I

Introduction

The Old Testament is a treasure trove of exciting history stories for you to explore with your students. *Pillars of History* is a unique, highly effective program that is easy to use for teachers as well as students. This book contains 24 lessons. Activities, questions, clear directions, and pictures are included to help facilitate learning. Each lesson will take one to five days to complete, depending on the setting.

The program utilizes highly effective methods of learning. Students not only gain knowledge of the Jewish Nation, but will see how to apply this knowledge.

Specially designed *3D Graphic Organizers* are included for use with the lessons. These organizers review concepts while adding to your students' understanding and retention of the subject matter.

This *Pillars of History* book is divided into four parts:

1. Following this *Introduction* you will find the *How to Use This Program* section. It contains all the information you need to make the program successful. The *How to Use This Program* section also contains instructions for Dinah Zike's *3D Graphic Organizers*. Please take the time to learn the terms and instructions for these learning manipulatives.

2. In the *Teacher's Section,* the numbered lessons include the Scripture, memory work, and activities that reinforce the concepts. Each activity includes a list of materials needed, directions, pictures, questions, written assignments and other helpful information for the teacher.

   The *Teacher's Section* also includes instructions for ongoing projects, as well as enrichment activities, entitled *Experiences, Investigations, and Research.*

3. *Graphics Pages,* listed by lesson numbers, provide pictures and graphics that can be used with the activities. They can be duplicated and used on student-made manipulatives, or students may draw their own illustrations. (Common Sense Press grants permission for you to photocopy the *Graphics Pages* for your students.)

4. The *Appendix* includes directions for making a set of *Keys to the Past* books, hosting a *Palestine Party,* constructing a *Hebrew Village,* and building a *Model Tabernacle.* (Common Sense Press grants permission for you to photocopy the *Keys to the Past* and *Model Tabernacle* patterns for your students.)

How to Use This Program

This program can be used in a single level classroom, multi-level classroom, homeschool, co-op group or Sunday School. You will find Scripture passages to read, verses to memorize, and projects for your students to make. These are meant to be the framework for your study, while you elaborate on concepts that are important to you. This is up to each parent or teacher. The Scripture will be your guide, as you teach each story and character.

First, look through the entire book. Become familiar with the *Teacher Pages* and *The Graphics Pages*.

Teaching the Lessons
Teacher preparation time for each lesson is minimal. Begin by reading through the Scripture. Then choose the activities your students will complete and gather the materials needed.

Introduce the lesson to the students by reading the Scripture together. Discuss the characters and what happened to them in the story. Talk about the lessons the people in the story learned. Then follow the directions for the *Graphic Organizers* and *On-Going Projects*. Choose an activity or two from *Experiences, Investigations, and Research*. Your week might look something like this:

Monday:	Read the Scripture and discuss.
Tuesday:	Make the *Graphic Organizer*.
Wednesday:	Work in *Timeline Book, Map Book,* and/or *Prayer Journal*.
Thursday:	Choose from *Experiences, Investigations, and Research*.
Friday:	Say memory verse. Choose from *Experiences, Investigations, and Research*.

Remember, this is only a suggested plan and should be adapted to suit your situation. If you find you have extra time, you may have a review day, or choose an extra project from the *Experiences, Investigations, and Research* section.

How to Use the Multi-Level Approach

The lessons in this book include basic content appropriate for grades K-8 at different mastery levels. For example, throughout the teaching process, a first grader will be exposed to much information but would not be expected to retain all of it. In the same lesson, a sixth grade student will learn principles at a deeper level, be able to communicate them in writing, and apply the principles to life.

The Scripture, which embodies the lesson, may in some cases be too lengthy for your younger students to pay attention to. Let them draw while you read, since your older students need to hear the whole passage. You may skim over the passage, reading excerpts appropriate for your student's listening ability. In some cases, you may substitute a children's story book, explaining that the story book is based on a real adventure taught in the Scripture.

In the Activities sections, icons are used to designate the levels of specific writing assignments.

This icon ✎ indicates the Beginning level, which includes the non-reading or early reading student. This level applies mainly to kindergarten and first grade students.

This icon ✎✎ is used for the Primary level. It includes the reading student who is still working to be fluent. This level is designed primarily for second and third graders.

This icon ✎✎✎ denotes the Intermediate level, or fluent reader. This level of activities will usually apply to fourth through eighth grade students.

If you are working with a student in seventh or eighth grade, we recommend using the assignments for the Intermediate level, plus at least one *Experiences, Investigations, and Research* activity per lesson.

No matter what grade level your students are working on, use a level of written work that is appropriate for their reading and writing abilities. It is best for students to review data they already know, learn new data and concepts, and be exposed to advanced information.

Experiences, Investigations, and Research

At the end of each lesson in the *Teacher's Section* is a category of activities entitled Experiences, Investigations, and Research. These activities expand upon concepts taught in the lesson, provide a foundation for further study of the content, or integrate the study with other disciplines. The following icons are used to identify the type of each activity.

Scriptures

Computer

Hands On

Writing

History

Literature

Research

Reading

Prayer Journal

Using 3D Graphic Organizers

The *3D Graphic Organizers* provide a format for students of all levels to conceptualize, analyze, review, and apply the concepts of the lesson. The *3D Graphic Organizers* take complicated information and break it down into visual parts so students can better understand the concepts. Most *3D Graphic Organizers* involve writing about the subject matter. Although the content for the levels will generally be the same, assignments and expectations for the levels will vary.

Beginning students may dictate or copy one or two "clue" words about the topic. These students will use the written clues to verbally communicate the Scripture lesson. The teacher should provide various ways for the students to restate the lesson. This will reinforce the lesson and encourage the students in their reading and higher order thinking skills.

Intermediate students may write several sentences or a paragraph about the topic. These students are also encouraged to use reference materials to expand their knowledge of the subject. As tasks are completed, students enhance their abilities to locate information, read for content, compose sentences and paragraphs, and increase vocabulary. Encourage these students to use the research skills to enhance their understanding of the Bible lesson.

Illustrations for the *3D Graphic Organizers* are found on the *Graphics Pages* and are labeled by the lesson number and a letter, such as 5A. Your students may use these graphics to draw their own pictures, or cut out and glue them directly on their work.

Several of the *3D Graphic Organizers* will be used over a series of lessons. For this reason, you will need a storage system for each student's *3D Graphic Organizers*. A pocket folder or a reclosable plastic bag works well. See page viii for more information on storing materials.

Ongoing Projects

Memory Work

Students have a memory verse each week. Say it together daily. Older students may write their verses on 3" x 5" cards that have been cut in half. For younger children, make verse charts by writing the verse for them on a quarter sheet of poster board. Let the children decorate the chart, or use illustrations. Punch a hole in the corner and keep all charts on a metal ring. At the end of the lesson, have the students say their verse from memory. As you work through the unit, review all verses for better retention.

Map Books

Map Books are designed to closely follow what happens in the Scripture stories. Map Book 1 is constructed in Lesson 1 and will be used through Lesson 10. Map Book 2 is constructed in Lesson 11 and will be used through Lesson 24. As children use an atlas to plot points on the map, they begin to see the reality of the Scriptures. Ask someone who visited the Holy Land to tell your students about their adventures.

TimeLine Book

In Lesson 2 an Accordion Book is made for a Timeline. This gives students a feel for what was going on in the world at the time of their Bible stories. In most lessons instructions are given for adding to the Timeline Book. The timeline figures are located in the *Graphics Pages*. Each timeline figure is numbered to match the corresponding lesson. Students glue the figure in the appropriate place, then draw a line from the picture to the correct time on the line. Encourage students to complete independent research and add other archaeological finds to the Timeline Books. Archaeology books and websites are excellent sources.

Passport Book Cumulative Project

Students construct a Passport Book to store the Graphic Organizers made during the studies. Do not overlook this project, as it provides immeasurable benefits for your student. Students will review all the content as they create the project. Each student organizes the material, providing an opportunity for authentic assessment and reinforcing the context in which it was learned. This project creates a format where students can make sense of a whole study in a way that cannot be accomplished otherwise.

Keys to the Past

Keys to the Past are twelve small books your students make to enhance this study. Students may work together to make a set for the family or each student may want his own set. Photocopy the pages or use the pages right out of the book to make your books. *Keys to the Past* may be constructed as you move through the study or all at once at the beginning of the study. Students will enjoy making their own reading and reference material.

Keys to the Past are not used for every lesson. Note the following chart:

Lesson Title		*Keys to the Past Titles*
Lesson 3.	Adam and Eve Disobey God	The Books of Moses - *Keys #1*
Lesson 4.	Cain and Abel	How the Torah Came to Us - *Keys #2*
Lesson 5.	Noah Found Grace	Ancient Architecture - *Keys #3*
Lesson 7.	Job	Seasons of the Year - *Keys #4*

Continued on next page

Timeline Figure Summary

Lesson/Graphic:	Timeline Figure:
1	None
2	Make the Timeline Book
3	None
4C	Creation
4D	First People
4E	Adam and Eve Leave the Garden
4F	First Murder
5E	Worldwide Flood
5F	8000 B.C. Cave painting in France
5G	2400 B.C. Worldwide Flood "Myth," Sumer
6	None
7K	2000 B.C. Job
7L	5000 B.C. Early Pottery, Turkey
8B	2000 B.C. Ox-Cart Model, Pakistan
8C	5300 B.C. Ziggurat, Sumer
8D	2000 B.C. Abraham
8E	5000 B.C. City of Ur Established
9B	3500 B.C. Early Jewelry: Gold Necklace
9C	5650 B.C. Early Sculpture: Idols, Catal Huyuk
9D	1896 B.C. Isaac Born
10B	1836 B.C. Jacob
11G	4000 B.C. Cylinder Seal, Sumer
11H	2500 B.C. Trade Routes, Crete
11I	1745 B.C. Joseph, Palestine
12A	3118 B.C. History Records: List of Kings, Egypt
12B	2600 B.C. Pyramids, Egypt
13C	1300 B.C. Moses' Birth, Egypt
13D	4000 B.C. Paper Making, Egypt
14C	3000 B.C. Irrigation, Egypt
14D	1300 B.C. Library at Amarna, Egypt
15	None
16E	1200 B.C. The Exodus, Egypt
16F	1670 B.C. Hyksos Chariot
17	None
18B	4000 B.C. Cuneiform, Sumer
18C	3000 B.C. Heiroglyphics, Egypt
19M	3000 B.C. Stonehenge, Britain
20C	8500 B.C. Jericho Founded
20D	2500 B.C. Town Planning, Pakistan
21E	6000 B.C. Scythe, Jordan
21F	6000 B.C. Spear, France
22B	8000 B.C. Jericho Wall Built, Canaan
22C	1800 B.C. Civilization begins in China
22D	3300 B.C. Civilization begins in India
23A	2100 B.C. Ur-Nammu writes earliest Code of Laws, Sumer
23B	1700 B.C. Hummurabi's Code
23C	1491 B.C. Mosaic Code, Mt. Sinai
24A	2100 B.C. Ancient Chinese Star Chart
24B	2100 B.C. Astronomy in Babylon

Fast Food and Fast Folds

"If making the manipulatives takes up too much of your instructional time, they are not worth doing. They have to be made quickly, and they can be, if the students know exactly what is expected of them. Hamburgers, Hot Dogs, Tacos, Mountains, Valleys, and Shutter Folds can be produced by students, who in turn use these folds to make organizers and manipulatives." – Dinah Zike

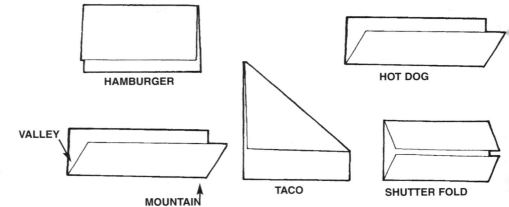

Every fold has two parts. The outside edge formed by a fold is called the **"Mountain."** The inside of this edge is the **"Valley."**

HAMBURGER · HOT DOG · VALLEY · MOUNTAIN · TACO · SHUTTER FOLD

Storage – Book Bags

One–gallon reclosable plastic bags are ideal for storing ongoing projects and books students are writing and researching.

Use strips of clear, 2" tape to secure 1" x 1" pieces of index card to the front and back of one of the top corners of a bag, under the closure. Punch a hole through the index cards. Use a giant notebook ring to keep several of the "Book Bags" together.

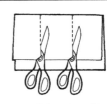

Label the bags by writing on them with a permanent marker.

Alternatively, the bags can be stored in a notebook if you place the 2" clear tape along the side of the storage bag and punch 3 holes in the tape.

3 Tab Book

1. Fold a sheet of paper in half like a Hamburger or Hot Dog.
   Fold it into thirds. Cut up the inside folds to form three tabs.

Pizza Book

Glue Graphic 1A-1H to sheets of card stock. Cut the card stock along the edge of each graphic.

Using clear packaging tape, tape together as follows:

1. Place H and G next to each other with H on the right. Tape the seam between them, leaving 1/8" gap. Leave this gap between each page as you tape, or the book will not shut properly.

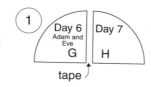

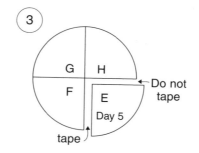

2. Place F to the left of G. Tape the seam.

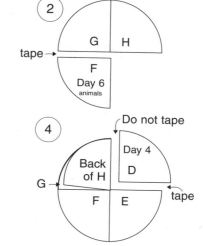

3. Place E to the right of F and tape the seam between E and F only.

4. Fold H over G to get it out of the way, then place D to the left of E and tape the seam of D and E only.

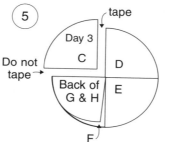

5. Fold H and G over F. Place C to the left of D and tape the seam.

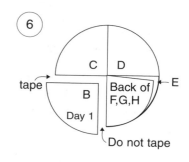

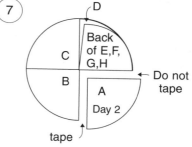

6. Fold H, G, and F over E. Place B to the left of C and tape the seam.

7. Fold H, G, F, and E over D. Place A to the right of B and tape the seam.

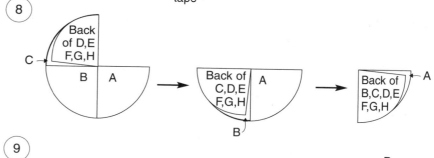

8. Fold H, G, F, E, D, C, and B over A.

9. Flip the whole book over and title it: *God Made the World.* (The title will be on the back of Graphic A. All other pages are blank on the back.) Now the book may be opened to reveal the student's work, beginning with Graphic A. Close the book in a spiral fashion.

Paper Hinges

A paper hinge is a method for securing 3D Graphic Organizers into the cumulative project. Hinges make it possible to layer 3D Graphic Organizers. Top ones can be lifted so student's work underneath may be viewed.

Cut a 1.5" strip of card stock or heavy paper, the same length as the width of the 3D Graphic Organizer to be secured. Fold the strip in half lengthwise. Glue one side of the "mountain" to the 3D Graphic Organizer, and the other side to the cumulative project.

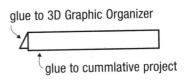

glue to 3D Graphic Organizer

glue to cummlative project

Large Question and Answer Book

1. Fold a sheet of paper in half like a Hamburger. Fold it in half again like a Hamburger. Make a cut up the Valley of the inside fold, forming two tabs.

2. A larger book can be made by gluing Large Question and Answer Books "side–by–side."

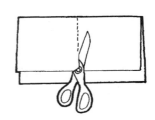

Pocket Book

1. Fold a sheet of paper in half like a Hamburger.

2. Open the folded paper and fold one of the long sides up 2 1/2" to form a pocket. Refold along the Hamburger fold so that the newly formed pockets are on the inside.

3. Glue the outer edges of the 2 1/2" fold with a small amount of glue.

4. Make a multi–paged booklet by gluing several Pocket Books "side–by–side."

5. Glue a construction paper cover around the multi–paged pocket booklet.

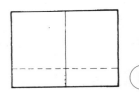

Accordion Book

1. Use five sheets of paper 12"x18". Fold one end of each sheet into a 1"tab. Sheets are now 12"x17", excluding this tab.

2. Fold each 12"x17" sheet into a Hamburger. Fold again into a Hot Dog. There should be four "pages" measuring 4 1/4"x12". Refold as needed to form an Accordian Book section as shown.

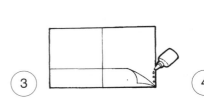
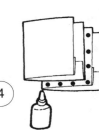

3. Glue sections together to make an Accordian Book by gluing a straight edge of one section into the tab-valley of another section. Cut off the extra tab at one end of the Accordian Book.

Note: Stand the sections on end and form an accordion with them before gluing. (See illustration.)

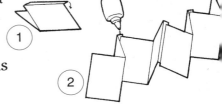

4 Door Book

1. Fold a sheet of paper into a Shutter Fold.

2. Fold it into a Hamburger.

3. Open the Hamburger and cut the Valley folds on the Shutters only, creating four tabs.

   Refold it into a Hamburger, with the fold at the top.

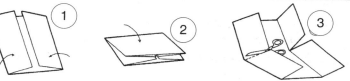

Layered Look Book

1. Stack two sheets of paper and place the back sheet one inch lower than the front sheet.

2. Bring the bottom of both sheets downward and align the edges so that all of the layers or tabs are the same distance apart.

3. When all tabs are an equal distance apart, fold the papers and crease well.

4. Open the papers and glue them together along the Valley/center fold.

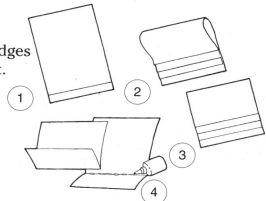

Matchbook

1. Fold a sheet of paper like a hamburger, but fold it so that one side is 1/2 to 1 inch longer than the other side.

2. Fold the one inch tab over the short side forming a matchbook-like fold.

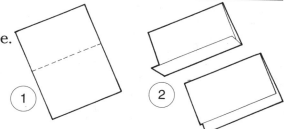

Envelope Fold

1. Fold a sheet of paper (8 1/2" x 11") into a taco forming a square. Cut off the excess paper strip formed by the fold.

2. Open the folded taco and refold it the opposite way forming another taco and an X fold pattern.

3. Open the taco fold and fold the corners toward the center point of the X forming a small square.

4. Cut 1" off of each point.

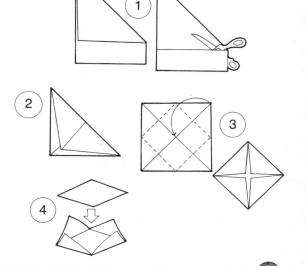

Side-by-Side

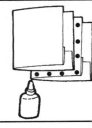

Some books can easily grow into larger books by gluing them side-by-side. Make two or more of these books. Be sure the books are closed, then glue the back cover of one book to the front cover of the next book. Continue in this manner, making the book as large as needed. Glue a cover over the whole book.

Billboard Project

1. Fold all pieces of the same size of paper in half like *hamburgers*.

2. Place a line of glue at the top and bottom of one side of each folded billboard section and glue them edge-to-edge on a background paper or project board. If glued correctly, all doors will open from right to left.

3. Pictures, dates, words, or symbols go on the front of each billboard section. The base, or the part glued to the background, is a good place for more in-depth information or definitions. Use for timelines or sequencing data.

Panorama Projects

1. Think of a scene, setting, or an object that is representative of the project.

2. Determine what will be to the foreground, midground, and background of your scene, setting, or object.

3. Using four pieces of paper or poster board, draw the foreground on one and cut around it. Draw the midground on another and cut around it. Draw the background on the last sheet and cut around it. Place all three cut sheets on top of the remaining whole sheet.

   Note: *If you are drawing a scene or setting, draw the foreground toward the bottom of the first sheet of paper. Cut this out. Since the midground needs to be drawn above the foreground, place the foreground illustration on top of the midground paper before drawing. Cut out the midground. The background should be drawn above the foreground and the midground, so place both the foreground and midground illustrations on the final page before drawing the background.*

4. Along the left side, staple or glue the three sheets of paper onto the solid sheet of paper so that they open like a book.

5. Glue data, illustrations, essays, short stories, poems, maps, etc., inside the project so they do not show when the project is closed. Information can also be glued onto the back sheet.

Teacher's Section

Internet Search Engines are used in Pillars of History as a gateway to investigation and research. Due to the changing nature of the Internet, we encourage teachers to preview the websites prior to assigning them to students.

The authors and publisher have made every reasonable effort to ensure that the experiments and activities in this book are safe when performed according to the book's instructions. We further recommend that students undertake these activities and Internet research under the supervision of a teacher, parent, and/or guardian.

God Creates The World

Scripture Reading: Genesis 1

Memory Verse: ✎ ✎✎ Genesis 1:1 or Ecclesiastes 3:11
✎✎✎ Isaiah 48:13

Activities:

Creation

Focus Skills: sequencing, describing stages
Paper Handouts: 8 sheets of 8.5" x 11" card stock   a copy of Graphics 1A-H
clear packaging tape
Graphic Organizer: Make a Creation Pizza Book. Glue Graphics A-H on card stock. Cut on the dotted lines. Assembly directions on page ix. Title the book *God Made the World*.

✎ Copy or dictate clue words along the top curve of each page such as: *Light, Water and Air, Land and Plants, Solar System, Birds, Sea Animals, Man and Woman, Animals Rest.* Color the pictures.

✎✎ Write clue words along the top curve of each page, such as: *light out of nothing, God spoke, firmament, atmosphere, dry land, plants that reproduce with seeds, after their own kind, solar system, birds of the air, undersea animals, man from the dust, woman from man, breath of life, in His own image, etc.* Color the pictures.

✎✎✎ Write a short summary at the top of each page using three or four sentences. List a key Scripture reference for each day of Creation.

Ongoing Project - Maps Top Tab Book 1: Ancient Civilizations

Focus Skill: following directions
Paper Handouts: a copy of graphics 1I-L
Graphic Organizer: Cut Graphics 1I-L. Stack and staple to form a Top Tab Book. With the Top Tab Book closed, write/copy the title *Maps of Ancient Civilizations* on the front. Label the first tab *Map Book 1*. Label the second tab *Ancient World*. Label the third tab *Fertile Crescent*. Label the fourth tab *Abraham's Journey*.

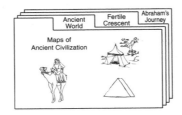

Teacher's Note: *Store this project for future use.*

Experiences, Investigations, and Research

Select one or more of the following activities for individual or group enrichment projects. Allow students to determine the format in which they would like to report, share, or graphically present what they have discovered. This should be a creative investigation that utilizes your students' strengths.

 1. Make a man of clay.

 2. Cut out magazine pictures of things God made. Glue to posterboard and write your Scripture verse at the bottom.

 3. Look up the definition of *ex nihilo*. Compare with man's artistic (or electronic, architectural, musical, mathematical and scientific) creations.

 4. Research the canopy theory. Where was it located? How might a canopy have affected man's life span?

 5. Think about the order of the Creation week. Write a paragraph explaining why you think God created the world in the sequence He did, using several examples. Glue the paragraph to the back of your Pizza Book.

 6. Research world religions to find out their beliefs about the origin of life.

The First People

Scripture Reading: Genesis 2

NOTE: *Help your children see the beautiful harmony that existed between these three beings (Genesis 3:8). Discuss God's one rule for Adam and Eve (Gen 2:16-17).*

Memory Verse: Genesis 1:27

Activities:

God, Adam and Eve

Focus Skill: explaining functions

Paper Handouts: 2 sheets of 8.5" x 11" paper   a copy of Graphics 2A-B

Graphic Organizer: Make two Hot Dog Books. (See instructions on page viii.) Make each fold on the left. Cut one into a 3 Tab Book. Turn the book so the fold is on the left. Glue Graphic 2A and 2B to the top and middle tabs of the 3 Tab Book. Work will continue on these in the next lesson.

Hot Dog Book:

✎ Write *GOD* in the front center of the Hot Dog Book. Use gold pen or decorate as desired with glitter. Inside, write *Creator*.

✎✎ Complete ✎. Inside, write the description of the Creator. Clue words: *creates out of nothing.*

✎✎✎ Complete ✎. Open the Hot Dog Book. On the left side, one word above the other, write *TIME, SPACE,* and *MATTER.* On the right side, use Genesis 1:1 to write a phrase across from each word showing that God created each: *In the beginning, God created the heavens, God created the Earth.*

3 Tab Book about Adam and Eve:

✎ Write the names beneath each picture. Under Adam's tab, draw a picture of the Garden of Eden. Under Eve's tab, draw a picture of Eve with Adam.

✎✎ Complete ✎. Inside, below your drawing of Adam, write *of the ground.* Below your drawing of Eve, write *Mother of all living.* These are the meanings of their names. Write about the special way they were created by God.

✎✎✎ Write the names beneath the pictures. Under Adam and Eve's tabs, write a description of the creation of each, as well as a "job description" for each. For Adam, see Genesis 3:8–*fellowship,* Psalm 29:1-2–*worship and praise,* Isaiah 43:7–*for My Glory,* and Genesis 1:28–*to replenish the earth and subdue it.* For Eve, see Genesis 1:27–*equality, image of God* and Genesis 2:18–*helper and companion.*

Teacher's Note: *Store these books for use in the next lesson.*

Hot Dog Book   3 Tab Book

Timeline Book

Focus Skill: following directions
Paper Handouts: 5 sheets of 12" x 18" paper   a copy of Graphics 2C-2L
Graphic Organizer: Make an Accordion Book (See page x) using
6 sheets of paper. This is the Timeline Book. Glue Graphic
2C on the middle of the first page of the Accordion Book.
Glue 2D at the middle of the second page of the Accordion
Book. Continue with Graphics 2E-N on the remaining
pages. Each 1000 year time period will use two time line
strip graphics. Store this project for future use.

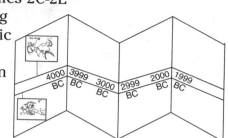

Teacher's Note: *Experts have different opinions about dates, and
archaeologists keep learning more. All dates given on timeline
graphics are an approximation.*

Maps Book 1: The Ancient World

Paper Handouts: Map Book 1
Graphic Organizer: Color the cover as
desired. Use an atlas to locate the
following. Label each on the *Ancient
World map*:
  Rivers: Tigris, Euphrates, Jordan,
  Nile, Nile Delta
  Cities: Babylon, Ur
  Region: Babylonia, Egypt
  Seas: Mediterranean Sea, Red Sea,
  and Persian Gulf

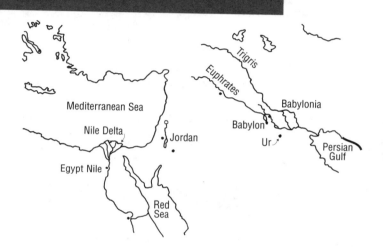

Experiences, Investigations, and Research

Select one or more of the following activities for individual or group enrichment projects.
Allow students to determine the format in which they would like to report, share, or
graphically present what they have discovered. This should be a creative investigation that
utilizes your students' strengths.

1. Look at wedding photos from your parent's wedding. Interview them about how
   they met and what life was like as newlyweds.

2. Draw a picture of your family. List things you are thankful for about your family.

3. Explain what you think it means that "man is made in God's image". (Genesis
   1:26) Write several paragraphs explaining your position. Include Genesis 9:6.

4. Research the treatment of women in other countries, especially in the Middle
   East and China.

Pillars of History, Part I

Adam and Eve Disobey God

Scripture Reading: Genesis 3

Memory Verse: Genesis 3:15

Activities:

Adam, Eve, and Satan

Focus Skill: explaining functions
Paper Handouts: a copy of Graphic 3A   3 Tab Book from Lesson 2
Graphic Organizer: Glue Graphic 3A to the third tab of the 3 Tab Book
✎   Write *Satan* beneath the graphic. Inside, write *Destroyer*.
✎✎   Complete ✎. Inside, describe how Satan tempted Eve. Clue words: *spoke through snake, questioned God's Words, cast doubt, said bad was good.*
✎✎✎ Write *Satan* beneath the graphic. Under the *Satan* tab, list three ways Satan tempted Eve.

Fall of Man

Focus Skill: application of information
Paper Handouts: 8.5" x 11" sheet of paper   a copy of Graphic 3B
Graphic Organizer: Make a 4 Door Book. Cut Graphic 3B on dotted lines and glue one on each tab.
✎   Open the tabs. Write/copy *sorrow, pain, sweat, death* on the inside of each door. In the center, write/dictate what happened to Adam and Eve after they disobeyed God.
✎✎   Complete ✎. Explain why God had to put Adam and Eve out of the Garden of Eden.
✎✎✎ Complete ✎✎. Explain the four aspects of the curse, using Genesis 3:16-19.

Encounter: Dramatization

Act out the story of Adam and Eve from their creation to their sin. Include their work in the garden, Satan's conversation with Eve, eating the fruit, hiding from God, and God's judgment on them. Show their emotions as they were tempted, afraid, and sorrowful as they had to leave the beautiful garden.

Experiences, Investigations, and Research

Select one or more of the following activities for individual or group enrichment projects. Allow students to determine the format in which they would like to report, share, or graphically present what they have discovered. This should be a creative investigation that utilizes your students' strengths.

1. Make a snake puppet out of a sock. Glue felt shapes, glitter, and wiggle eyes on if you like. Use the puppet to retell the story of Satan tempting Eve.

2. Research various interpretations of Genesis 3:15. Write a persuasive paragraph on one of these interpretations.

3. Another name for Satan is Devil, which means to divide. Research in the Scriptures other ways Satan caused division. **(Cain and Abel, 12 Spies, Job and his friends, Moses and the Children of Israel, David's sons)** Write several paragraphs explaining your conclusions.

4. The Laws of Thermodynamics are the most universal and best-proved generalizations of science. Research these laws and rewrite them in your own words in a Large Question and Answer book.

5. Construct and read *Keys to the Past #1* <u>The Books of Moses</u> located at the end of this book. See page 89.

6. Make a Prayer Journal. Make three Pocket Books. Glue them "Side-by-Side." Label each pocket as follows: *Obedient Servant, Promises of God, Awesome God, Faithful Father, Blessings, Prayer Requests.* You may want to cut a sturdy cardstock cover to glue around the front, spine and back. Write *Prayer Journal* on the front. Decorate as desired. Store the Prayer Journal for future use.

Cain and Abel

Scripture Reading: Genesis 4

Memory Verse: Genesis 4:9

Activities:

Cain

Cain and Abel

Focus Skill: comparing and contrasting
Paper Handouts: 8.5" x 11" sheet of paper   a copy of Graphics 4A-B
Graphic Organizer: Fold the sheet of paper into a Hot Dog and cut along the
fold. Make two Large Matchbooks about 4" x 5". Cut and color
Graphics 4A-B, glue each to a separate Matchbook. Write *Cain* on the
lower tab of Matchbook 4A. Write *Abel* on the lower tab of
Matchbook 4B.
Under the <u>Cain</u> *tab:*

Abel

✎   Write/copy *Farmer* on the inside top half. Draw his sacrifice on the
lower half. Under your picture, write a clue word such as *food, fruit or
grain.* Draw a sad face because God rejected this sacrifice.

✎✎   Complete ✎. Write a sentence about why God did not accept this offering from the
ground. HINT: Reread Genesis 3:17.

✎✎✎ Inside, write a paragraph about this man's life. See Genesis 4:5-17. Clue words:
vagabond, punishment, sign or mark, city.

Under the <u>Abel</u> *tab:*

✎   Write/copy *Shepherd* on the inside top half. Draw his sacrifice on the lower half. Under
your picture, write the word *Blood*, and draw a happy face because God accepted this
sacrifice.

✎✎   Complete ✎. Write a sentence about why God accepted this blood offering.

✎✎✎ Inside, write a paragraph about his short life. See Genesis 4:4. Clue words: *obedient,
prophet, respect, faith.*

Timeline

Paper Handouts: Timeline Book   a copy of graphics 4C-F
Graphic Organizer:
    4C Creation
    4D First People
    4E Adam and Eve Leave the Garden
    4F Pre-history First Murder

Cut Graphics 4C-F. Color if desired. Glue all four in the area called "Pre-history."
Discuss the meaning of the term "pre-history."

Experiences, Investigations, and Research

Select one or more of the following activities for individual or group enrichment projects. Allow students to determine the format in which they would like to report, share, or graphically present what they have discovered. This should be a creative investigation that utilizes your students' strengths.

 1. Study paintings of Creation, Adam and Eve, and Cain and Abel in story books or art books of the Middle Ages and Renaissance. Discuss the paintings. Make your own painting of one of these stories.

 2. Construct and read *Keys to the Past #2* How the Torah Came to Us. See page 89.

 3. Read Genesis 4:22. Research the Bronze Age and Iron Age. Consider Tubal Cain's occupation in light of this research. Write two paragraphs explaining your conclusions.

 4. On an index card write a prayer to God asking Him to help you in an area where you are tempted not to obey. Store this in the *Obedient Servant* pocket of your Prayer Journal. Write two or three prayer request cards, listing people you will pray for this month. Pray for these needs and place in the *Prayer Request* pocket. (See Lesson 3, Activity 6, for Prayer Journal directions.)

Noah Found Grace

Scripture Reading: Genesis 6:1 through Genesis 9:19

(This is a long passage and is repetitive in places. Use your judgment as you help your students get the most out of it.)

Memory Verse: Genesis 6:8, 9:6

Activities:

Noah and the Flood

Focus Skills: summarizing, retelling

Paper Handouts: 8.5" x 11" sheet of paper   a copy of Graphics 5A-D

Graphic Organizer: Make a Hot Dog 3 Tab Book. Cut, color, and glue Graphic 5A-C to the three tabs to form one picture. Turn over the 3 Tab Book. Glue 5D to the far left of the back of the book. Fold along right edge of 5D so it overlaps 5B on the front. Do all your writing under the tabs.

Under the left tab:

✎ Write/copy *Man turned against God.* Draw an angry face.

✎✎ Write a sentence about the people during Noah's time.

✎✎✎ Read Genesis 6:5-12 and write it in your own words.

Under the middle tab:

✎ Write/copy *Safe in the ark.* Draw eight people.

✎✎ Write sentences about how the animals came and how long the flood lasted. Draw eight people.

✎✎✎ Summarize Genesis 7:7-8:19.

Under the right tab:

✎ Write/copy *God's Promise* and draw a rainbow.

✎✎ Write a sentence about God's promise, using Genesis 9:8-17. Draw a rainbow.

✎✎✎ Summarize Genesis 9:8-17.

Timeline

Paper Handouts: Timeline Book   a copy of graphics 5E-G

Graphic Organizer:

5E Pre-history	Flood
5F 8000 B.C.	Cave Painting in France
5G 2400 B.C.	Worldwide Flood "Myth," Sumer

Cut out Graphics 5E-G. Color if desired. Glue to the appropriate places in the Timeline Book. Draw a line from the graphic to the timeline.

Paper Handouts: Maps Book from Lesson 1
Graphic Organizer: Use an atlas to locate and label the following on your *Fertile Crescent* map:
Rivers: Tigris and Euphrates
Cities: Babylon, Ur
Region: Mesopotamia. Write the meaning of Mesopotamia in small letters at the bottom of the map.
Other Geographical points of Interest: Syrian Desert, Mt. Ararat, Mediterranean Sea, Negev Desert

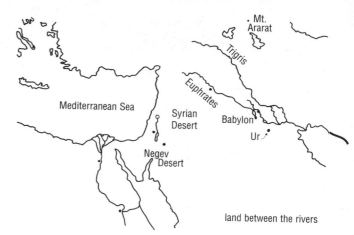

Experiences, Investigations, and Research

Select one or more of the following activities for individual or group enrichment projects. Allow students to determine the format in which they would like to report, share, or graphically present what they have discovered. This should be a creative investigation that utilizes your students' strengths.

 1. Glue colorful yarn into a rainbow shape on light blue construction paper. Write Genesis 9:13 across the bottom of the page. Draw Noah and his family praising God.

 2. Go outside and measure the length of the ark. See Genesis 6:15.

 3. Flatten a ball of clay into a slab. Press bones, shells, plastic dinosaur bodies or footprints into it, then remove. Allow to dry. Research how fossils are formed.

 4. Research the meanings of the names of Noah's sons. Find out which people groups each son became the "father" of. Write several paragraphs explaining your investigations.

 5. Research why some animals were taken in by sevens instead of twos. Explain your conclusions in a Hamburger Book.

 6. Watch the video "The Search for Noah's Ark."

 7. Construct and read *Keys to the Past #3*: Ancient Architecture.

 8. Think of a time you obeyed even though it was hard. Write this story on an index card. Thank God for His help, and place the card in the *Obedient Servant* pocket of your Prayer Journal.

Tower of Babel

Scripture Reading: Genesis 11:1-9

Memory Verse: Psalm 19:1

Activities:

Tower of Babel

Focus Skills: summarizing, evaluating

Paper Handouts: one half sheet of paper (8.5" x 5.5")   a copy of Graphic 6A

Graphic Organizer: Make a Shutter Fold. Cut and color Graphic 6A. Carefully cut it in half along dotted line. Glue each half on the front of the Shutter Fold. Write *Tower of Babel* under the graphic. Open the Shutter Fold. On the inside middle section:

✎   Write/copy a clue word such as *scatter, confusion, many languages, etc.*

✎✎   Explain why the people built the tower and what God did to change their plans.

✎✎✎ Summarize the story. Include possible reasons for building it, materials used, attitude of the people, God's judgment and its results. What command of God's were these people refusing to obey? (See Genesis 9:1, 7 and Genesis 1:28)

Encounter: Animal Babel Game

Materials: 12-20 people   small pieces of paper

How to Play: Write animal names on the papers. Have at least two papers per animal name. If you have more than 20 people, have three papers with the same animal. Pass out the papers and ask that players read them silently. At a signal, all players begin milling around, making the sound of the animal on their paper. They must find their fellow animals and pair off away from the group. Try both a loud and a soft version of the game, mixing and re-drawing new animal names. Talk about the confusion at Babel as people began to search for anyone who could understand their language.

Teacher's Note: *If you are playing with non-readers, you may pass out cards with animal pictures on them.*

Focus Skills: following directions, summarizing, reviewing
Paper Handouts: 1 sheet of dark color poster board
    7 plain or colored file folders, tabs trimmed
    a copy of Graphic 6B-F   Graphic Organizers from Lessons 1-6
Graphic Organizer: Glue file folders "Side By Side" to form a Passport Book. (See page xii.)

<u>**Passport Cover:**</u> Cut a piece of poster board 12" x 18 3/4". This is the passport book cover. Wrap the 12" x 18 3/4" piece of poster board around the *Passport Book.* Fold carefully, creating a spine. Remove the folded cover. Put plenty of glue along the spine only of the *Passport Book,* smearing with your finger for good coverage. Insert *Passport Book* into the folded passport cover, making sure the glued spine area has good contact with the spine of the cover. Secure with clothespins overnight until thoroughly dry. Cut and glue Graphic 6B-F to front. Title as desired.

<u>**Storage Pockets:**</u> Using the poster board scraps, cut two pieces 9" x 5". Position one piece against the lower half of the inner front cover, forming a pocket. Trim to fit if necessary. Run a thin line of glue down the side, across the bottom, and up the side of each piece. Glue in place, forming a pocket on the inside front cover. Repeat for the inside back cover. When dry, store the *Creation Pizza Book* in the front cover pocket. Enjoy reviewing your lessons.

<u>**Passport Book:**</u> Refer to page 15 for diagram.
1) Glue *GOD Hot Dog Book* and *Adam, Eve, and Satan 3 Tab Book* side by side onto page 1. Turn the page.
2) Glue *Fall of Man 4 Door Book* to center of page two.
3a) Glue *Cain and Abel Large Matchbooks* to the upper half of page three.
3b) Fold the *Noah 3 Tab Book* so that the third section is folded over the center section. Glue back of section one and two beneath the *Cain and Abel Matchbooks.* Leave the third tab folded over the center one. Turn the page.
4a) Glue *Tower of Babel Shutter Fold* to upper half of page four.
4b) Glue *Maps Top Tab Book 1* on lower half of page four.

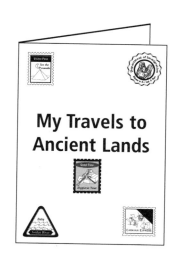

Experiences, Investigations, and Research

Select one or more of the following activities for individual or group enrichment projects. Allow students to determine the format in which they would like to report, share, or graphically present what they have discovered. This should be a creative investigation that utilizes your students' strengths.

 1. Study pictures of ancient ziggurats in a dictionary or encyclopedia. Build one in the sandbox.

 2. Research the Sumerian ziggurat. Record your research in a Large Question and Answer Book.

 3. Investigate ancient cultures that built magnificent huge structures. What do they all have in common? What was the purpose of each? Record your findings in Matchbooks.

 4. The ancient culture of Babylon was surprisingly sophisticated. Research the plumbing of ancient cultures.

 5. Most scholars agree the Tower of Babel was a ziggurat. The Hebrew word used in Genesis is "migdal" meaning a round tower. Write several paragraphs explaining the reasons the Tower of Babel was constructed.

Passport Book Assembly

These first four pages and cover of the Passport are constructed in Lesson 6.

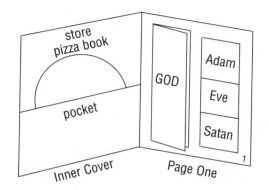

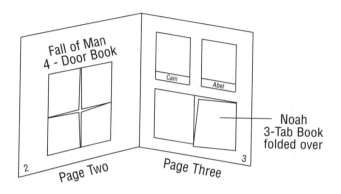

Noah
3-Tab Book
folded over

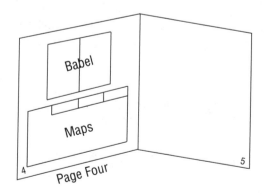

Teacher Note: The next assembly phase occurs
during Lesson 10, as shown on page 25.

Job

Scripture Reading:
Job 1   Satan's 1st attack and Job's response
Job 2:1-10   Satan's 2nd attack, Wife's Advice, Job's response
Job 2:11-13   Eliphaz, Bildad, and Zophar's Grief

Note: *Skim the rest of the book, using subtitles to guide you. The rest of the book consists of the conversation Job has with his friends. Each friend tells Job a reason for his suffering. See 4:4-8 for Eliphaz' advice, 8:3-6 for Bildad's and 11:4-7 for Zophar's.*

Memory Verse:
Job 1:21b
Job 1:20-22, or parts thereof

Activities:

Job

Focus Skills: summarizing, sequencing, analyzing
Paper Handouts: scrap paper   paper   a copy of Graphics 7A-J
Graphic Organizer: Use scrap paper to cut 10 pieces that are 2.5" x 3". Fold each in half so the closed size of each booklet is 2.5" x 1.5". Use these to make a Billboard Project. See page xii. Cut Graphics 7A-J and glue in order to the fronts of booklets. Glue booklets A-E across the half sheet of paper. Glue booklets F-J directly below. Do all writing inside the booklets.

✎   Write/Copy clue words for each small billboard booklet: *Job loved GOD, donkeys and cattle killed, sheep and servants killed, camels and servants killed, children killed, Job praises God, Job's wife complains, 3 friends sit with Job, 3 friends correct Job, God comforts Job.*

✎✎   Complete ✎, including more information. For example, tell how the animals were killed, tell what Job's wife said, describe how his friends joined him silently at first. Tell what his friends said to him. Tell what happened to Job in the end.

✎✎✎ Use the Scripture to describe the events in Job's life. List the advice given him by his wife and each friend. On the last booklet, summarize God's conversation with Job in the last 4 chapters.

Maps Books 1: Ancient World

Paper Handouts: Maps Book 1
Graphic Organizer: Job lived in the land of Uz. Check Noah's family history in Genesis 10:21-23 for a clue about who originally settled this area. **(Shem's grandson, Uz.)** Lamentations 4:21a will help you locate the area on *The Ancient World map.* Label the area of Edom. **(Edom means Esau and is where Esau's descendants settled.)**

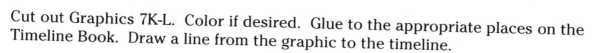

Paper Handouts: Timeline Book   a copy of Graphics 7K-L
Graphic Organizer:
   7K 2000 B.C.   Job
   7L 5000 B.C.   Early Pottery, Turkey

Cut out Graphics 7K-L. Color if desired. Glue to the appropriate places on the Timeline Book. Draw a line from the graphic to the timeline.

Experiences, Investigations, and Research

Select one or more of the following activities for individual or group enrichment projects. Allow students to determine the format in which they would like to report, share, or graphically present what they have discovered. This should be a creative investigation that utilizes your students' strengths.

1. **Teacher's Note:** *Parental help required for this activity.*
   Make two clothespin dolls of Job. Use the old-fashioned kind of clothespin without a spring. Drill a small hole through the shoulder place and insert a pipe cleaner for arms. Dress one Job in fancy fabrics with yarn bits for hair to show how he looked when he was rich. Dress the other Job in burlap and use a crayon to rub "ashes" on his clothes and head.

2. Research when the book of Job was written and by whom. Considering its age, how do you think it was preserved to eventually become part of the Scripture? **(Hint: Moses lived for forty years in Midian, not far from Uz.)**

3. The book of Job has more references to Creation, the Flood and other early Earth events than any other book, except Genesis. List some of the statements made by Job about God's created world.

4. Job is considered a masterpiece of literature, even by those who do not believe the Scriptures are the Word of God. What is the theme of the book of Job? Explain its lasting appeal in several paragraphs.

5. Job and his friends never mention the people of Israel, a Jewish nation, or any of the commandments of God. What does this seem to indicate? **(Job pre-dates Abraham.)**

6. Construct and read *Keys to the Past #4*, Seasons of the Year.

7. On an index card, write about a time you or someone you know suffered pain or sadness. List Scriptures that promise God's comfort in hard times. Store these in the *Promises* pocket of your Prayer Journal. On an index card, write three prayer requests for those you know in need. Pray for them and store the cards in the *Prayer Request* pocket of your Prayer Journal.

Pillars of History, Part I

Lesson 8

Abraham, Man of Faith

Scripture Reading: Genesis 12:1-9   The Journey
          Genesis 17:1-9   God's Covenant
          Genesis 18:1-16   The Visitors

Memory Verse: ✎ ✎✎   Genesis 12:2
            ✎✎✎   Genesis 12:2-3

Activities:

Life of Abraham

Focus Skills: summarizing, research, analyzing
Paper Handouts: 8.5" x 11" sheet of paper   a copy of Graphic 8A
Graphic Organizer: Make an Envelope Fold. Cut off 1" from the points in the center to create a blank square about 1 1/2" across. Glue Graphic 8A in this square space. Starting at the top tab and continuing clockwise, label the tabs *The Journey, The Visitors, Abraham Man of Faith* and *God's Covenant.* Open up all four tabs.
Teachers Note: *This is a detailed project. You may wish to do only one tab per day.*

Under The Journey tab:

✎   Draw a picture of Abraham and Sarah with their bundles. Add a camel or tent if you wish.

✎✎   Complete ✎. Explain why Abraham left his home. Clue words: *obeyed God, Ur, Haran, idol-worshippers, caravan.*

✎✎✎ Summarize Genesis 11:31, 12:1-9.

Under The Visitors tab:

✎   Draw Abraham by his tent. Draw three visitors talking to him.

✎✎   Complete ✎. Describe Abraham's visitors and the reason for their visit. Clue words: *baby, old age, miracle, laughed.*

✎✎✎ Illustrate as desired. Summarize Genesis 18:1-16.

Under Abraham Man of Faith tab:

✎   Write *Father of a Multitude* and draw a stone altar.

✎✎   Illustrate as desired. Copy Genesis 12:1.

✎✎✎ Illustrate as desired. Summarize Genesis 13:2, 8-9; Genesis 14:14-15.

Under God's Covenant tab:

✎   Use a cottom swab to smear glue. Add a bit of sand and some shiny stars.

✎✎   Illustrate as desired. Copy Genesis 12:2.

✎✎✎ Illustrate as desired. Summarize Genesis 13:14-18; 15:5-7, with 17-19.

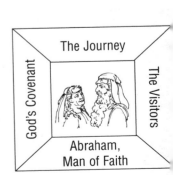

Maps Book 1: Abraham's Journey

Paper Handouts: Maps Book 1 in Passport Book.

Graphic Organizer: Use an atlas to locate and label the following on the map titled *Abraham's Journey:*
Cities: Ur, Haran, Bethel
Region: Canaan.
Trace: On *Abraham's Journey* page, trace Abraham's Journey from Ur to Haran to Bethel. Draw a tiny altar at Bethel. See Genesis 12:8.

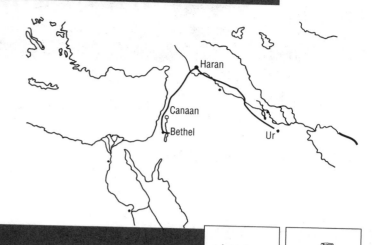

Timeline

Paper Handouts: Timeline Book   a copy of Graphics 8B-E
Graphic Organizer:

8B	2000 B.C.	Ox-Cart Model, Pakistan
8C	5300 B.C.	Ziggurat, Sumer
8D	2000 B.C.	Abraham
8E	3500 B.C.	City of Ur established

Cut out Graphics 8B-E. Color if desired. Glue to the appropriate places in the Timeline Book. Draw a line from the graphic to the timeline.

Experiences, Investigations, and Research

Select one or more of the following activities for individual or group enrichment projects. Allow students to determine the format in which they would like to report, share, or graphically present what they have discovered. This should be a creative investigation that utilizes your students' strengths.

1. Research the Bedouin people. Explain the ways their lives today are the same as they were in Abraham's time.

2. Check the encyclopedia for evidence Abraham really existed. Look under Abraham, Archaeology, Ur, etc.

3. Read God's promises to Abraham in Genesis 12:2-7. On a card describe God's faithfulness in keeping His promises. On a card describe God's faithfulness to you. Find a verse about faith and write it on a card. Store these in the *Faithful Father* pocket of your Prayer Journal.

Isaac, Son of Promise

Scripture Reading: Genesis 21:1-7 Birth
Genesis 22:1-19 Sacrifice
Genesis 24:1-67 Marriage

Memory Verse: ✎ ✎✎ Genesis 22:12b
✎✎✎ Genesis 22:12

Activities:

Life of Isaac

Focus Skill: summarizing
Paper Handouts: 8.5" x 11" sheet of paper   a copy of Graphic 9A
Graphic Organizer: Make an Envelope Fold. Cut off 1" from the points in the center to create a blank square about 1 1/2" across. Cut, color and glue Graphic 9A in this square space. Starting at the top tab and continuing clockwise, label the tabs *Saved from Sacrifice, Marriage, Isaac, Man of Promise,* and *Miracle Birth.* **Teacher's Note:** *This is a detailed project. You may wish to do only one tab per day.*

Under Miracle Birth tab:
✎ Draw a picture of old Abraham and Sarah with their new tiny baby.
✎✎ Complete ✎. Write a sentence about why Isaac's birth was so unusual. Clue words: *old age, prophecy, promise, fulfill.*
✎✎✎ Illustrate as desired. Summarize Genesis 21:5-7.

Under Saved from Sacrifice tab:
✎ Draw Isaac on the altar with Abraham standing near. Draw a ram caught in the bushes.
✎✎ Complete ✎. Describe the obedience test God gave Abraham. Clue words: *obedience, offer, sacrifice, provide, substitute.*
✎✎✎ Illustrate as desired. Summarize Genesis 22:2, 8, 10-13.

Under Marriage tab:
✎ Draw the servant bringing Rebekah home to Isaac.
✎✎ Complete ✎. Describe how God provided a wife for Isaac. Clue words: *servant, prayer, faith, willing.*
✎✎✎ Illustrate as desired. Summarize Genesis 24, especially verses 3-4, 10-14, 18-19, and 60-67.

Under Isaac, Man of Promise tab:
✎ Draw Isaac as a young man next to his old father.
✎✎ Complete ✎. Copy Genesis 21:2.
✎✎✎ Illustrate as desired. Summarize Genesis 22:16-18.

Paper Handouts: Maps Book 1 in Passport Book
Graphic Organizer: On the *Abraham's Journey* map, trace the route Abraham's servant must have taken. (Genesis 24:10–Nahor was probably somewhere near Haran.)

Timeline

Paper Handouts: Timeline Book   a copy of Graphics 9B-D
Graphic Organizer:

9B 3500 B.C.	Early Jewelry: Gold Necklace
9C 5650 B.C.	Early Sculpture: Idols, Catal Huyuk
9D 1896 B.C.	Isaac Born

Cut Graphics 9B-D. Color if desired. Glue to the appropriate places on the Timeline Book. Draw a line from the graphic to the timeline.

Experiences, Investigations, and Research

Select one or more of the following activities for individual or group enrichment projects. Allow students to determine the format in which they would like to report, share, or graphically present what they have discovered. This should be a creative investigation that utilizes your students' strengths.

1. Investigate the meaning of your name. On a piece of art paper, write your name in large letters. Write the definition below it in smaller letters. Decorate the border of the paper with drawings of family members, hobbies, favorite foods, friends' faces, your pet, favorite books, etc.

2. Use a concordance to find any verses that mention the word *name*. Look them up and copy some of the phrases you find in a Large Matchbook. Title your Matchbook *Importance of a Name.*

3. On a 3" x 5" card describe why Isaac was such a blessing to his parents. On several other cards, list some ways you can be a blessing to others. Store these in the *Blessings* pocket of your Prayer Journal.

Jacob, Man of Two Names

Scripture Reading:

Genesis 27:1-46	The Deception
Genesis 28:10-22	Dream at Bethel
Genesis 29	Two Wives
Genesis 32:22-32	Two Names

Memory Verse: Jeremiah 29:11

Activities:

Life of Jacob

Focus Skill: summarizing

Paper Handouts: 8.5" x 11" sheet of paper   a copy of Graphic 10A

Graphic Organizer: Make an Envelope Fold. Cut off 1" from the points in the center to create a blank square about 1 1/2" across. Glue Graphic 10A in this square space. Starting at the top tab and continuing clockwise, label the tabs *Dream at Bethel, Four Wives and Twelve Sons, Jacob, Man of Two Names* and *Brother Esau.*

Teachers Note: *This is a detailed project. You may wish to do only one tab per day.*

Under Brother Esau tab:

✎   Draw a picture of Jacob and Esau with the pottage.

✎✎   Complete ✎. Explain the differences between Jacob and Esau. Clue words: *hunter, rebellious, revengeful, hairy.*

✎✎✎ Illustrate as desired. Summarize Genesis 25:27, 34; 26:34-35; 27:41.

Under Dream at Bethel tab:

✎   Draw Jacob sleeping on a stone pillow with a ladder of angels nearby.

✎✎   Complete ✎. Describe Jacob's dream. Clue words: *ladder, angels, God, Abraham's covenant.*

✎✎✎ Illustrate as desired. Summarize Genesis 28:12-16.

Under Four Wives and Twelve Sons tab:

✎   Draw a numeral 4 and a numeral 12.

✎✎   Complete ✎. Copy Genesis 35:11-12.

✎✎✎ Illustrate as desired. Summarize Genesis 29;35:23-26

Under Jacob, Man of Two Names tab:

✎   Draw Jacob walking with a limp.

✎✎   Complete ✎. Copy Genesis 32:28.

✎✎✎ Illustrate as desired. Summarize Genesis 32:28; 35:10-15.

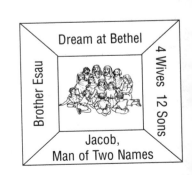

Passport Book Assembly

Focus Skill: following directions

Paper Handouts: Graphic Organizers constructed during Lessons 7-10
  Passport Book constructed in Lesson 6

Graphic Organizer: (Refer to page 25 for diagram.)

1) Glue the half sheet with *Story of Job Billboard Project* on the upper half of page 5 in the Passport Book. Turn the page.

2) Stack all three Envelope Folds on page 6. The *Abraham Envelope Fold* should be on top, then *Isaac,* then *Jacob.* Slide them apart slightly, so the bottom label of each Envelope Fold is showing. Leave a border above and below, as shown. When certain of arrangement, lift off top two Envelope Folds and glue the remaining *Jacob Envelope Fold* in place. Glue a Paper Hinge to the top back of the *Isaac Envelope Fold.* See page x. Glue a Paper Hinge to the top back of the *Abraham Envelope Fold.* Glue the Isaac hinge above the *Jacob Envelope Fold*, then glue the Abraham hinge above the *Isaac Envelope Fold.* They should lift up so the Envelope Fold beneath can be read. Enjoy reviewing all the lessons.

Teacher's Note: *Store for future use.*

Maps Book 1: Abraham's Journey

Paper Handouts: Maps Book 1

Graphic Organizer: On the *Abraham's Journey* map, trace the route Jacob must have taken as he fled from Esau. Draw a tiny ladder at Bethel. At Haran, draw Uncle Laban's tent. Label Penuel and draw Jacob and Esau meeting. Mark Hebron and draw old Isaac's tent.

Timeline

Paper Handouts: Timeline Book   a copy of Graphics 10B
Graphic Organizer:
  10B 1836 B.C.   Jacob

Cut Graphics 10B. Color if desired. Glue to the appropriate place on the Timeline Book. Draw a line from the graphic to the timeline.

Experiences, Investigations, and Research

Select one or more of the following activities for individual or group enrichment projects. Allow students to determine the format in which they would like to report, share, or graphically present what they have discovered. This should be a creative investigation that utilizes your students' strengths.

1. Research early hunters. Investigate the weapons and tactics that were successful for hunting game on foot.

2. Locate the meanings of the names Jacob and Esau. Explain the significance of the meanings.

3. Genesis 28:18 tells how Jacob made a pillar, or marker, so he would always remember what God had promised him. He also gave the place a special name. Ask your parents to tell you about their own spiritual "pillars."

4. Construct and read *Keys to the Past #5* <u>Nomadic Life.</u>

5. Jacob realized at Bethel what an awesome God he served. Use several index cards to list things He alone can do, things that amaze you. Pray, praising God for the reasons you listed on the cards. Store these in the *Awesome God* pocket of your Prayer Journal.

Passport Book Assembly

These next two pages of the passport are constructed in Lesson 10.

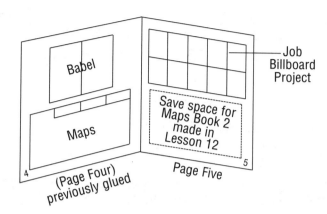

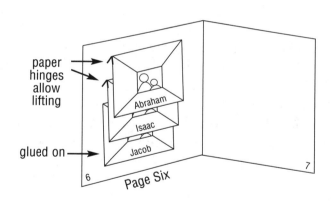

Teacher Note: The next assembly phase occurs
during Lesson 15, and is shown on page 45.

Joseph, The Dreamer

Scripture Reading: Genesis 37:1-11   Joseph's Two Dreams
Genesis 37:12-36   Joseph Sold into Slavery
Genesis 39:1-23   Potiphar and Prison

Memory Verse: ✎   ✎✎   Genesis 39:23b
✎✎✎   Genesis 39:5b

Activities:

Joseph, the Dreamer

Focus Skills: outlining, evaluating

Teacher's Note: Use brightly colored paper for the Layered Look Book or color stripes for the tabs to look like Joseph's many-colored coat.

Paper Handouts: 3 sheets of 6" x 11" paper   a copy of Graphic 11A

Graphic Organizer: Use the three sheets of paper to make a Layered Look Book with 1" tabs. Cut out pattern 11A. Glue the Layered Look Book to 11A on the designated line. Trim as needed to fit on Graphic 11A. Label the lower edges of the pages as follows, starting with the top tab: *Joseph's Coat, Joseph's Dream, Sold Into Slavery, Joseph in Prison, Pharoah's Dream, Joseph, the Ruler*. The first three tabs will be used in Lesson 11.

On Joseph's Coat tab:

✎   Draw a picture of Joseph's coat.

✎✎   Complete ✎. Write about Jacob's special love for Joseph. Gen. 37:3.

✎✎✎ Illustrate as desired. Explain Jacob's special love for Joseph (Genesis 37:3, 30:22-24) and Joseph's role in his father's life (Genesis 37:2).

On Joseph's Dream tab:

✎   Draw what Joseph saw in his dream.

✎✎   Complete ✎. Explain what Joseph's family thought when Joseph told them his dream. Why did they get angry?

✎✎✎ Explain the prophetic meaning of Joseph's dream as well as the symbolism.

On Sold into Slavery tab:

✎   Draw Joseph being thrown into the pit.

✎✎   Complete ✎. Describe what the brothers did to fool their father and hide their sin. See Genesis 37:22, 31-32.

✎✎✎ List the chain of events for Joseph from the pit to Potiphar. Explain how Joseph's brothers deceived their father.

Joseph's Coat
Joseph's Dream
Sold into Slavery
Joseph in Prison
Pharoah's Dream
Joseph, the Ruler

Focus Skill: following directions

Paper Handouts: a copy of Graphics 11B-F

Graphic Organizer: Cut graphics 11B-F. Stack and staple to form a Top Tab Book. With Top Tab Book closed, write/copy the title *Journey of God's Chosen People* on the front. Write *Joseph's Journey* on the first tab. Write *Israel in Egypt* on the second tab. Write *The Wilderness* on the third tab. Write *The Promised Land* on the fourth tab.

Teacher's Note: *Store this project for future use.*

Timeline

Paper Handouts: Timeline Book   a copy of Graphics 11G-I

Graphic Organizer:

11G	4000 B.C.	Cylinder Seal, Sumer
11H	2500 B.C.	Trade Routes, Crete
11I	1745 B.C.	Joseph, Palestine

Cut Graphics 11G-I. Color if desired. Glue to the appropriate places on the Timeline Book. Draw a line from the graphic to the timeline.

Experiences, Investigations, and Research

Select one or more of the following activities for individual or group enrichment projects. Allow students to determine the format in which they would like to report, share, or graphically present what they have discovered. This should be a creative investigation that utilizes your students' strengths.

1. How was Reuben planning to save Joseph? When his plan failed, explain an alternate plan he could have put into action.

2. Research why the many-colored coat was an appropriate gift for a favored son.

3. Research where the Midianites originated. (Genesis 25:1-4)

4. Construct and read *Keys to the Past #6* <u>Travel and Trade</u>.

5. Use an index card to list ways God was faithful to Joseph. Now list ways God has been faithful to you and your family. Store these in the *Faithful Father* pocket.

Joseph, the Ruler

Scripture Reading: Genesis 39:1-20   Potiphar's Household, Imprisoned
Genesis 39:21-40:23   Prisoners' Dreams Interpreted
Genesis 41:1-57   Pharoah's Dream, Famine
Genesis 42-46   Joseph's Brothers in Egypt
(This is a long passage and can be condensed for small children.)

Memory Verse: Genesis 50:20

Activities:

Joseph in Egypt

Focus Skills: outlining, evaluating
Graphic Organizer: Layered Look Book from Lesson 11
On Joseph in Prison tab:
✎   Draw Joseph with the baker and the butler.
✎✎   Complete ✎. Write about Joseph's authority in the prison and his ability to interpret dreams. Clue words: *favor, prosper.*
✎✎✎ Illustrate as desired. Explain why Potiphar trusted Joseph so fully (Genesis 39:5-6). Explain why he was trusted so fully in prison (Genesis 41:22-23).
On Pharoah's Dream tab:
✎   Draw the skinny and fat cows and the thin and full ears of corn.
✎✎   Complete ✎. Write about the King's problem (Genesis 41:8), Joseph's interpretation Genesis (41:25-36), and Joseph's new job (Genesis 41:39-49). Clue words: *dream, famine, store, overseer.*
✎✎✎ Illustrate as desired. Summarize ✎✎. Explain where the interpretations of dreams come from. See Genesis 40:8.
On Joseph, the Ruler tab:
✎   Draw Joseph in his royal Egyptian clothes.
✎✎   Complete ✎. Describe what happened when Joseph's brothers came to ask for food. How did Joseph test them? What was Joseph's goal? Clue words: *spies, reconciliation.*
✎✎✎ Illustrate as desired. Summarize Genesis 42:18-24, 44:16.

Maps Book 2: Joseph's Journey

Paper Handouts: Maps Book 2
Graphic Organizer: Color the cover as desired. Use an atlas to help you locate and label the following on the second page titled *Joseph's Journey*:
Regions: Gilead, Goshen   River: Nile
Country: Egypt   Cities: Hebron, Dothan, Shechem
Trace Joseph's journey to Egypt. (See answer map on next page).

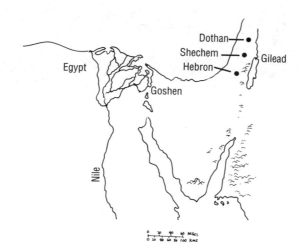

Egypt
Nile
Goshen
Dothan
Shechem
Hebron
Gilead

Paper Handouts: Timeline Book   a copy of Graphics 12A-B
Graphic Organizer:

12A	3118 B.C.	History Records: List of Kings, Egypt
12B	2600 B.C.	Pyramids, Egypt

Cut Graphics 12A-B. Color if desired. Glue to the appropriate places in the Timeline Book. Draw a line from the graphic to the timeline.

Experiences, Investigations, and Research

Select one or more of the following activities for individual or group enrichment projects. Allow students to determine the format in which they would like to report, share, or graphically present what they have discovered. This should be a creative investigation that utilizes your students' strengths.

1. Reread Judah's speech in Genesis 44:15-34. Explain what he is offering to do. (v.33)

2. Read David Macaulay's *Pyramids*.

3. Using an Internet Search Engine, research Ancient Egypt.

4. Investigate how mummies were made and why. Make a Small Question and Answer book to illustrate and record your findings. Notice Genesis 50:2,3, 26.

5. Using an Internet Search Engine, visit the Bread Beckers, research long term food storage.

6. Explain how Jacob and his extended family traveled to Egypt. How many miles was the trip?

7. God used Joseph's situation to bring about blessing. Think of times in your life when a situation looked hopeless, but God made something good to come of it. Tell about what happened on two or three index cards and store them in the *Blessings* pocket of your Prayer Journal.

Birth of Moses

Scripture Reading: Exodus 1   Summary of the plight of the children of Israel

Exodus 2:1-10   Moses' birth and adoption

Memory Verse: Genesis 2:10

Activities:

Moses is Born

Focus Skills: summarizing, sequencing

Paper Handouts: 8.5" x 11" sheet of paper   a copy of Graphic 13A-B

Graphic Organizer: Make a Large Question and Answer book. Glue Graphics 13A to the left tab and 13B to the right tab. Label Graphic 13A *Baby Moses.* Label Graphic 13B *Pharoah's Palace.*

Under Baby Moses tab:

✎   Draw Baby Moses in his mother's basket, floating in the Nile River.

✎✎   Complete ✎. Write/Copy about how Moses family tried to save him. Clue Words: *basket, pitch, Nile River, Pharoah's daughter, Miriam.*

✎✎✎ Using Exodus 2:1-4, describe the early events of Moses' life.

Under Pharoah's Palace tab:

✎   Draw paper and pen or a picture of Moses learning to write.

✎✎   Complete ✎. Write/copy about Moses' life in the palace. Clue Words: *teachers, writing, speak Egyptian, learn to be a Pharoah.*

✎✎✎ Write about Moses' life in the palace.

Maps Book 2: Israel in Egypt

Paper Handouts: Maps Book 2

Graphic Organizer: Work on the map titled *Israel in Egypt.* Trace the Nile River in blue. Research the meaning of delta. Color the delta lands green.

Timeline

Paper Handouts: Timeline Book   a copy of Graphic 13C-D

Graphic Organizer:

13C	1300 B.C.	Moses' Birth, Egypt
13D	2700 B.C.	Paper Making, Egypt

Cut out Graphics 13C-D. Color if desired. Glue to the appropriate places in the Timeline Book. Draw a line from the graphic to the timeline.

Experiences, Investigations, and Research

Select one or more of the following activities for individual or group enrichment projects. Allow students to determine the format in which they would like to report, share, or graphically present what they have discovered. This should be a creative investigation that utilizes your students' strengths.

1. Exodus 1:15-22 tells the story of Hebrew midwives who disobeyed Pharoah. God rewarded them. Discuss with your family about others who have lied to save lives.

2. Locate pictures of the buildings and monuments built in ancient Egypt. Research how long they took to build and what skills were needed. Build a minature of one of these, using dirt or clay.

3. Make a salt dough map of Egypt. Mix 3 cups of salt and 3 cups of flour thoroughly. Add 1 cup of water and stir evenly. Add more water if desired. Draw your map on heavy cardboard or a piece of plywood. Cover your drawing with dough, carving the Nile delta with a pencil and shaping the mountains along the Red Sea. Let it dry a week and then paint it. Use blue for bodies of water, green for fertile areas, and shades of brown for surrounding deserts.

4. On an index card list the names of new babies you know. Pray for them and store the cards in the *Prayer Request* pocket. Think about how faithful God was to baby Moses. Think of a time when you or someone you know was in great danger, and God saved them. Write what happened on an index card and store in the *Faithful Father* pocket of your Prayer Journal.

Moses, the Deliverer

Scripture Reading:
Exodus 2:11-15   Escape to Midian
Exodus 2:16-25   Moses finds a wife
Exodus 3:1-22   The calling of Moses

Memory Verse:
✎ and ✎✎   Exodus 3:17 (omitting tribal names after Canaanites)
✎✎✎   Exodus 3:15

Activities:

Moses, the Deliverer

Focus Skills: summarizing, researching
Paper Handouts: 8.5" x 11" sheet of paper   a copy of Graphics 14A-B
Graphic Organizer: Make a Large Question and Answer book. Glue Graphics 14A to the left tab and 14B to the right tab. Label Graphic 14A *Children of Israel*. Label Graphic 14B *Burning Bush*.

Under <u>Children of Israel</u> *tab:*
✎   Draw a brick or people making bricks.
✎✎   Write/copy about the hard life of God's people. Clue Words: *brick, mortar, bondage, treasure, cities.*
✎✎✎ Using Exodus 1:8-15, 22, describe what life was like for the children of Israel and why the Egyptians feared them.

Under <u>Burning Bush</u> *tab:*
✎   Draw a burning bush. Draw Moses with his shoes off.
✎✎   Write/copy what happened to Moses in the desert. Clue words: *bush, fire, didn't burn up, voice of God, holy ground.*
✎✎✎ Using Exodus 3: 15-22, outline God's instructions to Moses, including what God says will happen when His people leave Egypt.

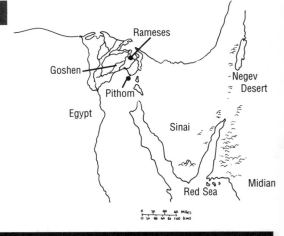

Maps Book 2: Israel in Egypt

Paper Handouts: Maps Book 2
Graphic Organizer: Use an atlas to locate and label the following on the map page titled *Israel in Egypt*.
<u>Cities and Regions:</u> Rameses, Midian, Pithom, Goshen, and Egypt
<u>Seas:</u> Red Sea
<u>Deserts:</u> Sinai Desert, Negev Desert

Paper Handouts: Timeline Book   a copy of Graphics 14C-D
Graphic Organizer:

    14C   3000 B.C.   Irrigation, Egypt
    14D   1300 B.C.   Library at Amarna, Egypt

Cut out Graphics 14C-D. Color if desired. Glue to the appropriate places in the Timeline Book. Draw a line from the graphic to the timeline.

Experiences, Investigations, and Research

Select one or more of the following activities for individual or group enrichment projects. Allow students to determine the format in which they would like to report, share, or graphically present what they have discovered. This should be a creative investigation that utilizes your students' strengths.

1. Review Lesson 12: how Joseph's family moved to Egypt with God's blessing (Genesis 46:3-4). Was their enslavement part of God's plan? Discuss with an adult how adversity can bind us to the heart of God.

2. Moses spent many years in Midian as a shepherd before God used him. Israel wandered many years in the desert before reaching Canaan, though there was a shorter route. Explain why you think God sometimes delays blessing His people.

3. Investigate survival in the desert. Make a list of your needs for a one month long desert trek.

4. What physical law of the universe did Moses know was being violated when he saw the Burning Bush? Explain Moses' response to this and why you think he responded in this manner.

5. Research the land of Egypt today: the family life, religion, dress, architecture and military. Record your findings in a Hamburger Book.

6. Construct and read *Keys to the Past #7* <u>Ancient Hebrew Clothing</u>.

Pharaoh Meets the One True God

Scripture Reading: Exodus 5:1-2   Pharoah's first chance to obey God
                    Exodus 6:1, and 7:1-11:10   The Ten Plagues
                    (This is a long passage and can be condensed for small children.)

Memory Verse: ✎ and ✎✎   Exodus 6:7
                    ✎✎✎   Exodus 6:7-8

Activities:

12 Plagues

Focus Skills: sequencing, analyzing

Paper Handouts: a copy of Graphic 15A

Graphic Organizer: Cut along dotted lines to form 12 Miniature Matchbooks. Fold each Matchbook along dashed lines.

✎   Draw a picture inside each matchbook, drawing a rod or scepter for Moses and Pharoah. Illustrate each plague.

✎✎   Complete ✎. Write/Copy a clue word for each plague: *dead fish, frogs in homes, bugs everywhere, dead cows, painful sores, strange storms, crops destroyed, dark all day, dead firstborn children, animals, Moses, and Pharoah.*

✎✎✎ Research Egyptian gods. Use the chart below to write the name and a characteristic of the Egyptian god which corresponds to each plague. Illustrate if desired. Write a character trait inside the Moses and Pharoah matchbook.

GOD's Battle with the gods of Egypt   *(See Numbers 33:4)*

Nile to blood	Sobek, god of crocodiles Khnum, controller god of the Nile	**Boils**	Isis, goddess of healing
		Hail	Nut, sky goddess
Frogs	Heqet, goddess of childbirth with the form of a frog	**Locusts**	Osiris, god of crops
		Darkness	Re, god of the sun
Gnats	Set, god of desert sands and storms	**Death of Firstborn**	Tawaret, protector of babies
Flies & Insects	Scarabaeus (beetle) was worshipped		Bes, protector of homes and children
Death of all Cattle	Hathor, depicted with head of a cow		

Paper Handouts: Maps Book 2
Graphic Organizer: Examine your map titled *Israel in Egypt* and imagine how the plagues occurred in the areas where Egyptians lived, but not in Goshen where the Israelites lived.

Passport Book Assembly

Focus Skills: following directions
Paper Handouts: Graphic Organizers from Lessons 11-15
Graphic Organizer: (Refer to page 45 for diagram.)
1) Glue the *Joseph Layered Look Book* from Lesson 11-12 to page 7.
2a) Glue the *Baby Moses* and *Pharoah's Palace Large Question and Answer Book* from Lesson 13 to the top half of page 8.
2b) Glue the *Children of Israel* and *Burning Bush Large Question and Answer Book* from Lesson 14 to the bottom half of page 8.
3) Glue the *12 Miniature Matchbooks* from Lesson 15 to page 9. (Optional: You may wish to mount the Miniature Matchbooks on a colorful piece of paper about 7 1/2" x 10" before gluing to page 9.)

Experiences, Investigations, and Research

Select one or more of the following activities for individual or group enrichment projects. Allow students to determine the format in which they would like to report, share, or graphically present what they have discovered. This should be a creative investigation that utilizes your students' strengths.

1. Research polytheistic religion. Compare and contrast this system with monotheism in a Large Question and Answer Book.

2. Each plague mocked an Egyptian god or goddess. Investigate the chief deity of Egypt. Explain why the plague of Darkness was one of the final two signs.

3. Research Egyptian Pharoahs. List examples of how they were treated as deity. Record your findings in a Matchbook.

4. Research the art of paper making. Try making homemade paper.

5. Construct and read *Keys to the Past #8* Egyptian gods.

6. Spend this week going through all the pockets in your Prayer Journal. Pray for requests, praise God, and be thankful.

Pillars of History, Part I
1491 B.C.
Lesson 16

Passover and the Red Sea

Scripture Reading:

Exodus 12:1-28	The First Passover Feast
Exodus 12:29-36	Death of the Firstborn
Exodus 12:37-42	Israel Leaves Egypt
Exodus 13:17-22	Pillar of Fire, Pillar of Cloud
Exodus 14	Israel crosses the Red Sea, Egyptians drowned
Exodus 15	Israel praises God

Memory Verse: ✐ and ✐✐   Exodus 15:2a
✐✐✐   Exodus 15:2

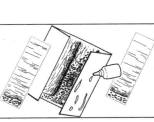

Activities:

Passover

Focus Skills: summarizing, sequencing
Paper Handouts: 8.5" x 11" sheet of paper   a copy of Graphics16A-B
Graphic Organizer: Make a Shutter Fold. Cut Graphic 16A in half and glue halves to outside doors of Shutter Fold. Glue Graphic 16B inside the Shutter Fold. On the outside, write/copy *Death Angel Passes Over.*

✐   Color the pictures. Color the blood on the door. Inside, draw a picture of a smiling, healthy firstborn child.

✐✐   Complete ✐. Write/copy the names of the Passover foods God said to eat: *roast lamb, bitter herbs, unleavened bread.*

✐✐✐ Explain the first Passover. See Exodus 12:5-8.

Crossing the Red Sea

Focus Skills: summarizing, sequencing
Paper Handouts: 8.5" x 11" sheet of paper
a copy of Graphics16C-D
Graphic Organizer: Make a Shutter Fold. Cut Graphic 16C in half and glue to outside of Shutter Fold. Title it *Crossing the Red Sea.* Glue Graphic 16D inside the Shutter Fold.

✐   Color the pictures. Inside, draw a picture of a child carrying a bundle.

✐✐   Complete ✐. Write/copy what happened when the Egyptians chased the Israelites into the sea. Clue Words: *chariots, horses, drowned, singing.*

✐✐✐ Summarize Exodus 14:21-31.

Maps Book 2: The Wilderness

Paper Handouts: Maps Book 2
Graphic Organizers: Use an atlas to speculate what part of the Red Sea the Israelites might have crossed. Mark this place on the map titled *The Wilderness.*

Paper Handouts: Timeline Book   a copy of Graphics 16E-F
Graphic Organizer:

| 16E | 1200 B.C. | The Exodus, Egypt |
| 16F | 1670 B.C. | Hyksos Chariot |

Cut out Graphics 16E-F. Color if desired. Glue to the appropriate places in the Timeline Book. Draw a line from the graphic to the timeline.

Experiences, Investigations, and Research

Select one or more of the following activities for individual or group enrichment projects. Allow students to determine the format in which they would like to report, share, or graphically present what they have discovered. This should be a creative investigation that utilizes your students' strengths.

1. Research how Passover is celebrated today. Talk to a Jewish person or view a Passover video. List the elements of the Passover meal and explain each one's significance.

2. On a paper plate, draw or use magazine pictures to illustrate Passover foods.

3. Watch Cecil B. DeMille's *The Ten Commandments* with Charlton Heston. Notice Hollywood embellishment, and locate where the movie is in line with Scripture.

4. Compare and contrast Miriam's song of praise in Exodus 15 to the words of the Israelites in Exodus 16:2-3.

5. Research the history of the chariot. Make a timeline of its use and changes throughout history.

6. Find Scriptures telling of God's promises when we are afraid. Jot down several verses on index cards, then thank God that He casts out fear. Write one more index card naming the awesome things God did for the Israelites. Store cards in the *Awesome God* pocket.

God's Care in the Desert

Scripture Reading: Exodus 13:17-22   Pillar of cloud, fire
                     Exodus 16:1-36   Manna, quail

Memory Verse: Exodus 13:21

Activities:

God's Care in the Desert

Focus Skills: summarizing, following directions

Paper Handouts: 1 sheet 8.5" x 11" brown paper   half sheet of deep blue paper
1 sheet 8.5" x 11" light blue paper   half sheet of tan paper
sesame seeds, optional   (Graphic 17 A-B)

Graphic Organizer: Make a Panorama Project:

<u>Back Page:</u> Take the sheet of light blue paper and fold it in a Hamburger. Open it and fold it in a Hot Dog. Open it so there are four squares. Color the top right square black. Set aside.

<u>Third Page:</u> Cut desert mountains across the top of the sheet of brown paper. About one fourth of the paper should be cut off in doing this. Lay this sheet on top of the blue page and adjust mountains as necessary. Line up lower edges of papers.

<u>Second Page:</u> Cut the top edge of the half sheet of deep blue paper into the curving shape of a river. Lay on top of the mountain page. Line up lower edges of papers.

<u>First Page:</u> Cut the top edge of the half sheet of tan paper into a river bank. Dot it with a crayon to look like manna or glue on sesame seeds. Stack up all pages forming a scene, and staple or glue along left edge. With book shut, glue Graphic 17A over the light blue square on the third page and Graphic 17B over the black square on the third page.

Back Page

Third Page

Second Page

First Page

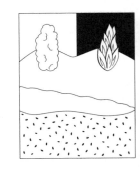

Completed
Panorama Project

Teacher's Note: *Drawings should be done with Panorama Project closed so they will show. Writing should be done carefully so that it cannot be seen when the Panorama Project is closed.*

Back Page:

✎ Write/copy *cloud* and *fire* next to each graphic. On the lower half, write/copy *God led His people.*

✎✎ Complete ✎. Write/Copy your memory verse.

✎✎✎ Compare Exodus 13:21 with Exodus 40:38 and I Kings 8:10-11. Write your conclusions.

Third Page:

✎ Close your Panorama Project. Draw tents at the "foot" of the mountains, along the water's edge.

✎✎ Complete ✎. Lift the second page and write/copy Exodus 13:20.

✎✎✎ Read Exodus 13:17-18. Lift the second page. Explain why God led his people through the wilderness of the Red Sea, rather than the shorter way.

Second Page:

✎ Draw wavy lines in the river. Lift the first page and write/copy *God gave water from a rock.*

✎✎ Complete ✎. Write about how God gave water to the people.

✎✎✎ Summarize Exodus 17:6.

First Page: (*Do all writing on the back of the first page.*)

✎ Draw specks of manna on the ground. Draw several small birds flying low over the ground. Write/copy *Manna* and *Quail.*

✎✎ Complete ✎. Write a sentence about God's rule for gathering manna. Exodus 16:13-17.

✎✎✎ Use Exodus 16 to explain God's provision for eating and for rest.

Experiences, Investigations, and Research

Select one or more of the following activities for individual or group enrichment projects. Allow students to determine the format in which they would like to report, share, or graphically present what they have discovered. This should be a creative investigation that utilizes your students' strengths.

1. Research the behavior of quail. List unusual behavior in the daily quail meals.

2. Read Deuteronomy 29:5 to learn about God's provision for clothes and shoes. Record your findings under the Mountain Page of the Panorama Project.

3. Numbers 33:1-56 is an account of the travels of the Israelites, including their camping places, and where they were when God gave them instructions for invading Canaan. Make a list of each location and explain why you think it was recorded in the Scriptures.

4. Think of ways God has shown His care for you. How has He supplied your needs? List them on a card and file under *Blessings*.

God Gives
Ten Commandments

Scripture Reading: Exodus 20:1-21

Memory Verse: The 10 Commandments

Activities:

The Ten Commandments	
I *You shall have no other gods before Me.*	VI *You shall not murder.*
II *You shall not make for yourself a false god or worship any other god but Me.*	VII *You shall not commit adultery.*
III *You shall not take the name of the Lord in vain.*	VIII *You shall not steal.*
IV *Remember the sabbath day, to keep it holy.*	IX *You shall not lie.*
V *Honor your father and your mother.*	X *You shall not covet your neighbor's house.*

Ten Commandments

Focus Skill: applying information
Paper Handouts: 3 sheets 8.5" x 11" paper   a copy of Graphic 18A
Graphic Organizer: Make two Hot Dog Books. Place next to each other so the folds are touching and the open edges are at the outsides. Cut Graphic 18A into 10 commandment strips plus a Title strip. Glue the first five Commandment strips in order on the lower half of the left Hot Dog Book. Glue the last five Commandment strips in order on the lower half of the right Hot Dog Book. Cut through top layer of each Hot Dog Book so each Commandment strip may be lifted independently. Cut a curve at the top of each Hot Dog Book so that together they resemble the tablets of stone. Glue the Hot Dog books next to each other on the third sheet of paper. Center and glue the Title strip just above the Commandments.

✎   Lift each Commandment and write/copy a phrase explaining each commandment in your own words.
✎✎   Complete ✎.
✎✎✎ Complete ✎. Write a sentence or two explaining each commandment.

Maps Book 2: The Wilderness

Paper Handouts: Maps Book 2
Graphic Organizer: Use your atlas to locate where we think Mt. Sinai might have been located. Sketch it on the map titled *The Wilderness*. There is a great deal of dispute about this.

Timeline

Paper Handouts: Timeline Book   a copy of Graphics 18B-C
Graphic Organizer:

18B	4000 B.C.	Cuneiform, Sumer
18C	3000 B.C.	Heiroglyphics, Egypt

Cut out Graphics 18B-C. Color if desired. Glue to the appropriate places on the Timeline Book. Draw a line from the graphic to the timeline.

Focus Skill: following directions
Paper Handouts: Graphic Organizers from Lessons 16-18
Graphic Organizer: (Refer to page 45 for diagram.)
1) Glue the *Passover Shutter Fold* from Lesson 16 to page 10.
2) Glue the *Crossing the Red Sea Shutter Fold* from Lesson 16 to page 11. Turn page.
3) Glue the *God's Care Panorama Project* from Lesson 17 to page 12.
4) Glue the *Ten Commandment Book* to page 13.

Experiences, Investigations, and Research

Select one or more of the following activities for individual or group enrichment projects. Allow students to determine the format in which they would like to report, share, or graphically present what they have discovered. This should be a creative investigation that utilizes your students' strengths.

 1. Make a poster of the 10 Commandments. Draw pictures around the edges showing how they apply in your life. Hang your poster in an important place in your home.

 2. Make tablets from bakable clay. Write the 10 Commandments in the clay with a toothpick or wooden skewer. Bake as directed.

 3. Construct and read *Keys to the Past #9* <u>Ancient Hebrew Food</u>.

 4. On an index card, write about a time you did not obey. Describe the consequences of your disobedience. Pray for help when obeying is hard. Keep the card in the *Obedient Servant* pocket.

A Tabernacle for God

Scripture Reading: Exodus 25:1 through 27:21

Memory Verse: ✎ and ✎✎ Exodus 40:34
✎✎✎ Exodus 40:38

Activities:

Tabernacle

Focus Skills: researching, defining

Paper Handouts: a sheet of 8.5" x 11" paper   a copy of Graphics 19A-L

Graphic Organizer: Cut along dotted lines to form 12 Miniature Matchbooks. Fold each Matchbook along dashed lines.

✎ ✎✎ Write/copy names of tabernacle furniture and people inside each Miniature Matchbook. Draw a picture about each part of the tabernacle.

✎✎✎ Complete ✎, in more detail. Example: Include Aaron's responsibilities, how the artisans embroidered the veil, how the metalworkers used wood, gold and brass. Explain the function of each piece of tabernacle furniture.

19A	Tabernacle	Exodus 25:8
19B	Aaron	Exodus 28:1
19C	Artisans/Metalworkers	Exodus 31:1-6
19D	Altar of Burnt Offering	Exodus 29:18, 42-46
19E	Laver	Exodus 30:18-21 with Psalm 51:2,7
19F	Altar of Incense	Exodus 30:7
19G	Lampstand	Exodus 27:20
19H	Table of Shewbread	Exodus 25:30
19I	Veil	Exodus 26:33
19J	Ark of the Covenant	Exodus 25:22
19K	Pillar of Cloud	Exodus 40:38
19L	Covering	Exodus 26:13

Store your Miniature Matchbooks to be used later.

Paper Handouts: Maps Book 2
Graphic Organizer: Use an atlas to locate the Wilderness of Sinai. Label it on *The Wilderness* map. Draw a tiny picture of the Ten Commandments "stone tablets" next to Mt. Sinai. Draw tiny tents in the Wilderness of Sinai to represent the Israelite camp.

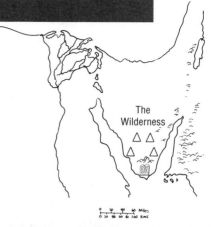

Timeline

Paper Handouts: Timeline Book   a copy of Graphic 19M
Graphic Organizer:

19M   3000 B.C.   Stonehenge, Britain

Cut out Graphic 19M. Color if desired. Glue to the appropriate place in the Timeline Book. Draw a line from the graphic to the timeline.

The Plan of the Tabernacle

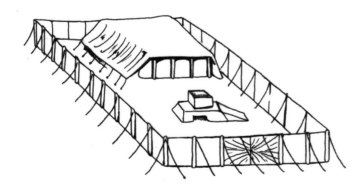

What a wonderful place for God to dwell among His people! Most of the time when we say "tabernacle," we mean the Holy Place and the Holy of Holies. The word "tabernacle" can also refer to the entire structure, including the curtained outer court.

Experiences, Investigations, and Research

Select one or more of the following activities for individual or group enrichment projects. Allow students to determine the format in which they would like to report, share, or graphically present what they have discovered. This should be a creative investigation that utilizes your students' strengths.

 1. Construct a model tabernacle using patterns and instructions in Appendix C.

 2. Compare and contrast the tabernacle of the Hebrew God to the worship places of other people groups (Mayan, Germanic tribes, Native American tribes). Report your findings in a Layered Look Book.

 3. Read Exodus 29:1-9. What part of this ceremony sounds familiar to you? (See 1 Samuel 16:11-13.) Explain why you think the anointing is significant.

4. After all the walls, furniture for the tabernacle, and clothes for the priests were completed, explain what happened next and why you think this occurred. Read Exodus 39:33-43.

5. Animals had to die so God could clothe Adam and Eve. Explain what priestly activity this foreshadowed.

6. Construct and read *Keys to the Past #10* Hebrew Feasts of the Lord.

7. On an index card, try to imagine what it must have been like inside the tabernacle. Can you picture the glowing candlelight reflecting in the gold Table of Shewbread, the Ark of the Covenant barely visible behind the beautifully embroidered curtain? Record your impressions of this holy place. On another card, write a few sentences of praise to God for His awesome power and holiness. Place the cards in the *Awesome God* pocket of your Prayer Journal.

Passport Book Assembly

These next three pages of the passport are completed in Lesson 15.

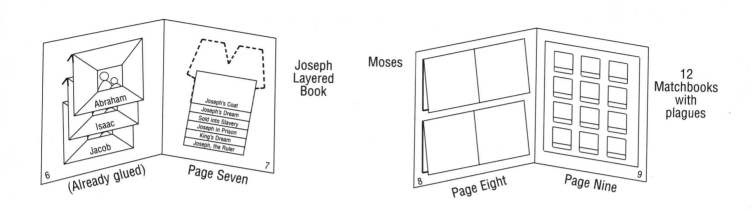

These next four pages are completed in Lesson 18.

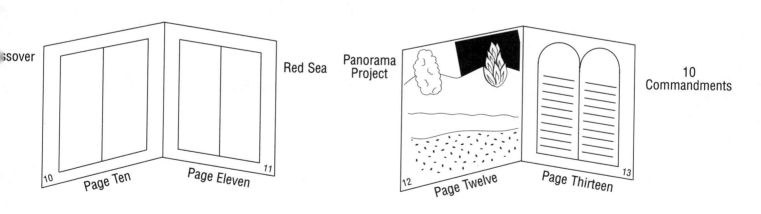

Teacher Note: The next assembly phase is after Lesson 24 on page 55.

Pillars of History, Part I

Twelve Spies

Scripture Reading: Numbers 13 and Numbers 14:1-39
(Note that in KJV, Joshua's name in 13:8 is Oshea)

Memory Verse: ✎ and ✎✎ Numbers 14:8
✎✎✎ Numbers 14:8-9

Activities:

Twelve Spies

Focus Skills: comparing and contrasting
Paper Handouts: a sheet of 8.5" x 11" paper   a copy of Graphics 20A-B
Graphic Organizer: Fold the sheet of paper into a Hot Dog and cut along the fold. Set aside
one half. Make a Shutter Fold with the other half. Glue Graphic 20A to the left side of
the shutter, and Graphic 20B to the right side. Write 10 Foolish Spies under the picture
of 10 men. Write 2 Faithful Spies under the picture of 2 men.

✎   Write/Copy *Fear* under the left flap. Write/Copy *Faith* under the right flap.

✎✎   Complete ✎. Under the left flap, explain why the 10 spies were afraid. Under the right
flap, explain why Joshua and Caleb wanted to take the land.

✎✎✎ Complete ✎ and ✎✎. Under the left flap, summarize the events that followed the lack
of faith. Under the right flap, summarize the reward God had for Caleb and Joshua.

Maps Book 2: The Promised Land

Paper Handouts: Maps Book 2
Graphic Organizer: Work on the map page titled *The Promised Land*. Use an atlas to locate
and label the following:
<u>Regions:</u> Moab and Canaan
<u>Bodies of Water:</u> Dead Sea, Jordan River, and Sea of Galilee

Map answers at Lesson 24.

Timeline

Paper Handouts: Timeline Book   a copy of Graphics 20C-D
Graphic Organizer:
20C   5500 B.C.   Jericho Founded
20D   2500 B.C.   Town Planning, Pakistan

Cut out Graphics 20C-D. Color if desired. Glue to the appropriate places in the
Timeline Book. Draw a line from the graphic to the timeline.

Experiences, Investigations, and Research

Select one or more of the following activities for individual or group enrichment projects. Allow students to determine the format in which they would like to report, share, or graphically present what they have discovered. This should be a creative investigation that utilizes your students' strengths.

 1. Research the agriculture of Israel today. Taste some of their fruits such as pomegranate, dates, and figs.

 2. Try your spy skills with a disguise, notebook, pencil, and binoculars. Take turns "trailing" each other. Record all movements of your "enemy."

 3. Make paper bag puppets of Caleb and Joshua. Draw their heads on a piece of paper. Cut across their faces at the mouth line. Glue the upper part of the face to the bottom of a paper bag. Glue the chin and lower part of mouth so it meets the upper part of the face. Make the puppets talk about the land they saw and how God will help Israel triumph over their enemies.

 4. Most of the time we think of God's promises being about His provision and His faithfulness. God also has promises concerning disobedience. Read Deuteronomy 8:19-20. What was His plan for the Israelites if they worshiped other gods? Write about this on a card. Pray and ask God to help you to obey Him. Place the card in the *Promises* pocket of your Prayer Journal.

Rahab Saves Two Spies

Scripture Reading: Joshua 1 and 2

Memory Verse: ✎ and ✎✎ Joshua 1:9
✎✎✎ Joshua 1:8-9

Activities:

Rahab and the Two Spies

Focus Skills: outlining, researching

Paper Handouts: a copy of Graphics 21A-D   2" piece of red thread

Graphic Organizer: Cut out Graphics 21A-D. Stack in order so 21A is on top. Staple in two or three places at the left side, forming a Side Tab Book. Title the book *Rahab Hides Two Spies*. Label the tab of 21B *The Mission*. Label the tab of 21C *Rahab Saves Two Spies*. Label the tab of 21D *God Spares Rahab*. Glue red thread "hanging" on one side of a wall.

On The Mission Page:

✎ Write/copy the words *Spy on Jericho*. Draw a picture of a walled city.

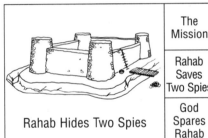

✎✎ Complete ✎. Write a sentence from Joshua 2:18-19.

✎✎✎ Complete ✎ and ✎✎. Using Joshua 2:3 explain the great risk these men were taking.

On Rahab Saves Two Spies Page:

✎ Write/copy the words *They hid under the flax*. Draw a picture of two men hiding under flax.

✎✎ Complete ✎. Write a sentence about the King's men. See Joshua 2:3-5.

✎✎✎ Complete ✎ and ✎✎. Explain the proposal Rahab made to the men. Include Rahab's apparent belief in the Hebrew God.

On God Spares Rahab Page:

✎ Write/copy the words *Rahab's family is safe*. Draw a picture of Rahab and her family.

✎✎ Complete ✎. Write a sentence about why God spared her.

✎✎✎ Complete ✎ and ✎✎. Explain why God would save a non-Hebrew.

Maps Book 2: The Promised Land

Paper Handouts: Maps Book 2

Graphic Organizer: Use an atlas to help you locate and label the following cities on *The Promised Land* map:
Cities: Jericho and Ai

Map answers at Lesson 24.

Paper Handouts: Timeline Book   a copy of Graphics 21E-F
Graphic Organizer:

21E	6000 B.C.	Scythe, Jordan
21F	6000 B.C.	Spear, France

Cut out Graphics 21E-F. Color if desired. Glue to the appropriate places in the Timeline Book. Draw a line from the graphic to the timeline.

Experiences, Investigations, and Research

Select one or more of the following activities for individual or group enrichment projects. Allow students to determine the format in which they would like to report, share, or graphically present what they have discovered. This should be a creative investigation that utilizes your students' strengths.

1. Read Joshua 2:9-11 to discover the reputation of Israel. Write a persuasive paper supporting Israel's reputation.

2. Read Joshua 2:18. The Hebrew word "line" KJV is usually translated as "hope" (see Psalm 71:5). What was Rahab's hope? What is the significance of the color of the thread she used in the window?

3. Research the uses of flax. Investigate how it is processed and why Rahab had so much of it on her roof.

4. Construct and read *Keys to the Past #11* <u>A Woman's Life</u>.

5. Think about your memory verse. What was God asking the Israelites to do? What was He promising them about Himself?   Describe a Faithful Father in your own words. Title a 3" x 5" card *Faithful Father* and write your thoughts down. Write on another 3" x 5" card about a time God has kept His promise to you. Place the cards in the *Faithful Father* pocket of your Prayer Journal.

Two Wicked Cities

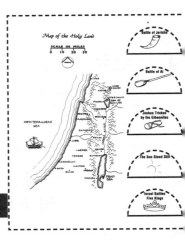

Scripture Reading: Joshua 6-8

Memory Verse: ✏ and ✏✏   Psalm 71:1

✏✏✏   Psalm 71:1-3

Activities:

Map Project With Tabs: Israel Enters Canaan

Focus Skills: map skills, sequencing

Paper Handouts: a sheet of card stock   a copy of graphic 22A

Graphic Organizer: Color Graphic 22A Map of Canaan as desired. Cut along dotted lines to form five tabs. Glue Graphic 22A to the sheet of card stock, keeping tabs free.

Under the Battle of Jericho Tab:

✏   Draw a pair of feet and a horn.

✏✏ and ✏✏✏ Write a short phrase about the battle of Jericho.

Under the Battle of Ai Tab:

✏   Draw the things Achan had taken and hid in his tent (Joshua 7:20-21).

✏✏ and ✏✏✏ Complete ✏. Write a phrase about what the Israelites did to Achan.

Maps Book 2: The Promised Land

Paper Handouts: Map Book 2

Graphic Organizer: Read Joshua 3:12-4:9, 4:20-24. Use an atlas to locate Gilgal, then label it on the map titled *The Promised Land*. Draw a tiny memorial of 12 stones next to it.

Map answers at Lesson 24.

Timeline

Paper Handouts: Timeline Book   a copy of Graphics 22B-D

Graphic Organizer:

22B	5000 B.C.	Jericho Wall Built, Canaan
22C	1800 B.C.	Civilization Begins in China
22D	3300 B.C.	Civilization Begins in India

Cut out Graphics 22B-D. Color if desired. Glue to the appropriate places in the Timeline Book. Draw a line from the graphic to the timeline.

Experiences, Investigations, and Research

Select one or more of the following activities for individual or group enrichment projects. Allow students to determine the format in which they would like to report, share, or graphically present what they have discovered. This should be a creative investigation that utilizes your students' strengths.

1. Due to its great wickedness, God intended for Jericho never to be rebuilt. He put a curse on any man who tried it. Read about this curse in Joshua 6:26 and see how it was fulfilled in I Kings 16:34. Record your findings in a Matchbook.

2. Compare your memory verse to Rahab's testimony. Her hope was in the scarlet cord and her life depended on the invading warriors keeping their promise when they saw it.

3. Construct and read *Keys to the Past #12* History Books.

4. Only after Achan, his family and his belongings were destroyed was the Lord able to turn from the "fierceness of His anger" (Joshua 7:25-26). Discuss why punishment for sin turns God's anger. On a index card, thank God for His forgiveness. Place the cards in the *Obedient Servant* pocket of your Prayer Journal.

Joshua is Tricked

Scripture Reading: Joshua 9

Memory Verse: ✎ and ✎✎ Psalm 19:14

✎✎✎ Psalm 19:13-14

Activities:

Map Project With Tabs: Israel Enters Canaan

Focus Skills: map skills, sequencing
Paper Handouts: Map Project from Lesson 22
Graphic Organizer:
Under the Joshua Tricked by the Gibeonites Tab:

✎ Draw a picture of a pair of old shoes and some moldy bread.

✎✎ Complete ✎. Explain why the Gibeonites wanted to fool Joshua. Tell about the bargain they made with Joshua.

✎✎✎ Complete ✎✎. How do you think this poor decision will affect Israel in the future? (Remember, all Canaanites were to be destroyed because of their evil idol worship.)

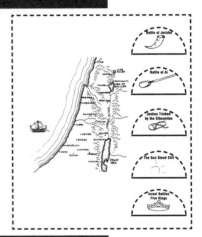

Maps Book 2: The Promised Land

Paper Handouts: Maps Book 2
Graphic Organizer: Use an Atlas to locate Gibeon. Label it on the map titled *The Promised Land.* Notice how close the Gibeonites were to Jericho and Ai. Draw a tiny shoe next to Gibeon.

Timeline

Paper Handouts: Timeline Book   a copy of Graphics 23A-C
Graphic Organizer:

23A	2100 B.C.	Ur-Namma of Ur writes earliest Code of Laws
23B	1700 B.C.	Hammurabi's Code, Babylon
23C	1491 B.C.	Mosaic Code, Mt. Sinai

Cut out Graphics 23A-C. Color if desired. Glue to the appropriate places in the Timeline Book. Draw a line from the graphic to the timeline.

Experiences, Investigations, and Research

Select one or more of the following activities for individual or group enrichment projects. Allow students to determine the format in which they would like to report, share, or graphically present what they have discovered. This should be a creative investigation that utilizes your students' strengths.

 1. Build a diorama depicting the story of Joshua meeting the Gibeonites. Dress clothespin dolls or other figures in ragged clothes and shoes. Design old wineskins and baggage to make them appear as travelers from afar. Add tents and cooking pots to represent Joshua's camp.

 2. Research optical illusions to find out how easily the eye can be fooled. Locate examples of several and share them with your family or friends.

 3. Research early laws. In a Large Question and Answer Book explain how Hammurabi's Code differs from the Mosaic Code.

 4. Use an index card to retell a time you had to pay a price for disobedience. On another card, describe the lesson you think Joshua had to learn. Think of several people you know who are in need. Describe their need on another card and then pray for them. Pray for the other requests you have written about before. Place the cards in the *Obedient Servant* and *Prayer Requests* pockets of your Prayer Journal.

The Sun Stands Still and Five Kings are Defeated

Scripture Reading: Joshua 10

Memory Verse: ✎ and ✎✎ Psalm 19:1
✎✎✎ Psalm 20:6-8

Activities:

Map Project With Tabs: Israel Enters Canaan

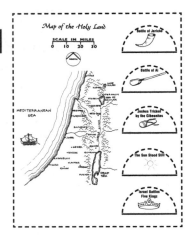

Focus Skills: map skills, summarizing
Paper Handouts: Map Project begun in Lesson 22
Graphic Organizer:
Under The Sun Stood Still Tab:
✎   Draw a bright shining sun. Next to it draw a clock. Draw a big X on the clock.
✎✎ and ✎✎✎ Complete ✎. Tell why God made the sun stand still (Joshua 10:12-14).
✎✎✎

Under Israel Battles Five Kings Tab:
✎   Draw five crowns.
✎✎ and ✎✎✎ Complete ✎. Write a phrase explaining how the five kings gathered against Israel.

Maps Book 2: The Promised Land

Paper Handouts: Maps Book 2
Graphic Organizer: Use an atlas to locate and label the
following on *The Promised Land* map:
Cities: Jerusalem, Hebron, (*Jarmuth, *Lachish, *Eglon)
Draw a tiny crown beside each one you are able to locate. Maps Book 2 is now complete and may be glued to the bottom half of page 5 in the Passport Book.
*The locations of these are in dispute and are uncertain. More archeological evidence is needed.

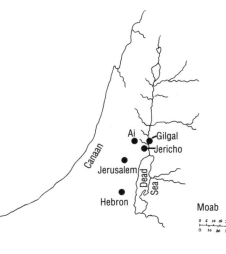

Timeline

Paper Handouts: Timeline Book   a copy of Graphics 24A-B
Graphic Organizer:

    24A   2100 B.C.   Ancient Chinese Star Chart
    24B   2100 B.C.   Astronomy in Babylon

Cut out Graphics 24A-B. Color if desired. Glue to the appropriate places in the Timeline Book. Draw a line from the graphic to the timeline. Take time now to review your Timeline Book. See if you can remember dates, people, inventions, etc. Make up your own Timeline Quiz questions for a Game Show.

Prayer Journal: Awesome God, Prayer Requests

Paper Handouts: Prayer Journal   3" x 5" cards
Journal Entry: At the top of a card, write *Only God Can:* and list several things that only God can do. You may be able to fill more than one card. Be sure to include a description of what He did for Joshua. Place the cards in the *Awesome God* pocket. Think of some people you know who need God's awesome power in their lives. Write a description of their needs on some 3" x 5" cards and pray for them. Place these cards in the *Prayer Requests* pocket of your Prayer Journal. (This project is for those who have been making the Prayer Journal throughout the unit.)

Passport Book Assembly

Focus Skills: Following directions
Paper Handouts: Graphic Organizers from Lessons 19-24
Graphic Organizer: (Refer to diagram below.)

    1)   Glue *12 Tabernacle Miniature Matchbooks* from Lesson 19 to page 14. (Optional: You may wish to glue the Miniature Matchbooks to a colorful piece of paper 7 1/2" x 10" before gluing to page 14.)
    2a) Glue the *12 Spies Shutter Fold* from Lesson 20 to the top half of page 15.
    2b) Glue the *Rahab Hides Two Spies Side-Tab Book* from Lesson 21 to the bottom half of page 15. Turn the page.
    3)   Glue the *Map Project With Tabs* from Lessons 22-24 to page 16.

Other Graphic Organizers made during this study may be stored in the pocket of the inside back cover. Enjoy reviewing your work.

Passport Book Assembly

The next four pages were completed in Lesson 24.

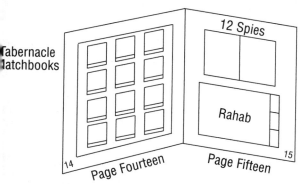

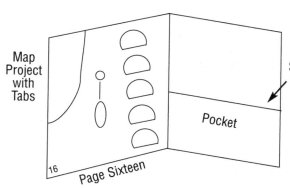

Notes

Host a Palestine Party

**Older students will enjoy helping younger children
put on this party. Don't forget the camera!**

Focus: Students experience what it was like to live in ancient times. Students experiment with the food, games, clothing and ways of life.

Costumes:

Ask your guests to come to the party dressed as people who lived in ancient Jewish times or as a specific character. Think of common people as well as kings and queens. The following are suggestions for simple costumes:

Head Covering:
- A towel and dad's old tie
- A pillow case: open the pillow case and fold it inside out until the opened ends touch the sewn end. Sew the opened ends to the pillow case at the sewn end. Put one corner of the pillow case on the child's head as a covering.
- cardboard crown with plastic jewels
- filmy veil or flowers
- plastic armor

Clothing:
- child's bath robe
- old pillow case with neck hole and armholes cut out
- plastic armor

Props:
- Carry a stuffed lamb and staff, basket with baby, lamp, stick horse, stones and sling, walking stick, plastic spear, market items, jewelry or coins.

Atmosphere:

Place rugs and big pillows on the floor. Hang pictures of ancient Hebrew life on the walls. Use pictures of heroes, the Tabernacle, Pharoah, Adam and Eve, Noah, etc. Have a few story books for children to look at until everyone arrives for the party. Play Jewish music softly in the background.

Outdoor Games:

All outdoor games require adult supervision.

Jump the river:
Use two ropes that are at least 6 feet long. Lay them on the ground parallel to each other, about a foot apart to represent a river. Line up the children and let them jump over the river without stepping into the "water." When all have jumped, move the

ropes apart a little. Let the children jump again. Keep moving the ropes apart. As children "fall" in the river, they are out. The game continues until the river is too wide for anyone to jump across without getting "wet."

Spear Toss:
Use a long stick for a "spear." Children take turns hurling it from a given spot. Throwers replace the spear with a marker (identifiable rock or stick). See who can throw the spear the farthest.

Chariot Races:
You will need two ropes 6' to 8' long. Children form pairs; one will be the horse and one will be the chariot driver. Place the rope center around the "horse's" tummy and let the driver hold both ends of the rope. Chariots begin at a designated starting line, drive round a distant point, and return to start. Race two chariots at a time, or more if you have more ropes. **(Historical note: The Israelite army did not have chariots. Jewish children who played a game like this were imitating chariots of their enemies. Perhaps their mothers made them stop!)**

Other games:
Hopscotch (A very old game with variations around the world.)
Jump Rope
Any game the children invent using natural materials

Food:

Place an old bedspread on the floor. Let the children sit in a circle around the edges. During the meal, let children talk about their favorite Scriptural stories and characters. To serve the meal, use paper plates in wicker plate holders or a cloth napkin for a "plate." Serve foods available in Palestine:

cheese (try goat cheese!)	olives
milk (try goat milk!)	raisins
apples, cut up	unleavened or pita bread
dates	butter
honey	pomegranate
figs	grapes

Cut the figs and dates into tiny pieces, encouraging children to "taste test" a new food. If figs are unavailable, fig cookies would let the children experience this fruit.

Homemade Butter:
Pour a pint of whipping cream into a jar. Ask the children to sit in a circle and take turns shaking the jar, passing the jar to the next person when their arms get sore. Keep shaking until butter appears. Stop the process every so often so all can see what is happening. When a solid lump of butter is swimming in "buttermilk", pour off the liquid and use the butter. Add salt if desired. **(Historical note: Salt was prized in Old Testament times for its ability to preserve and flavor food. In some places, salt was used like money for trading.)**

Unleavened Bread:

Buy Jewish Matzah bread. Find it at a Kosher deli or grocery store. All kinds of Jewish foods are available in grocery stores at Passover time.

Pita Bread:

2 c. hot water

2 tsp. honey

1 T. salt

4 c. flour

1 c. whole wheat flour

6 tsp. yeast

Preheat pizza stone to 500 degrees. Place ingredients in order into Bosch™ mixer bowl, using only half the flour at first. Turn on mixer and add flour until dough cleans sides of bowl. Knead for 6 minutes. Make balls that are about 1/2 c. dough. Let rest 10 minutes. Roll out each ball to 1/4" thick and let proof about 10-12 minutes. Bake directly on pizza stone for 5-7 minutes, turning over halfway through the baking time.

Note: No pizza stone? Use a cookie sheet. No Bosch? Use any mixer to begin, then remove dough and knead by hand 8 minutes. No doubt Sarah and Rachel had a baking stone on a fire, but certainly no Bosch.

Goat Cheese:

Let 1 qt. buttermilk sit out overnight. Set aside. Scald 1 gallon goat milk. Keep it going hot for 20 minutes without scorching. Turn off the heat and pour in the buttermilk. Let it sit a few minutes, then pour through a cheesecloth-lined colander. It will have the consistency of cream cheese.

Jacob's Pottage:

(Use your own recipe for lentil or pea soup, or try this favorite!)

2 c. lentils

4-6 c. water

2 t. minced garlic

1 T. dried minced onion

1 stalk celery, chopped

1 carrot, chopped

1 16 oz. can tomatoes

1 chicken boullion cube

2 T. minced parsley

1 t. salt

1/2 t. pepper

1 bay leaf

1/4 t. thyme

1 10 oz. pkg frozen chopped spinach

Combine lentils and water in a large pan. Bring to boil. Simmer uncovered for 15 minutes. Saute garlic, onion, carrot, and celery in a little oil until tender, about 5 minutes. Stir into lentils. Add tomatoes, boullion, parsley, and seasonings. Heat to boiling. Reduce heat, cover, and simmer 1 hour. Add spinach during the last 20 minutes. Remove bay leaf before serving. Makes enough for 12 children to try.

Craft:

Make scrolls using adding machine tape or strips of paper. Tape the ends to straws or popsicle sticks. Write a memory verse or Hebrew alphabet letters, then roll up and tie with yarn.

Departure:

Be sure to take a group picture before sending guests home. Everyone says "Shalom" to each other, wishing one another peace.

Make a Hebrew Village

**Your students will enjoy making all the tiny accessories for this model village.
Use materials you have on hand, and let your students get creative.**

Focus: Students use their creativity and research skills to make a diorama of a village from ancient times.

Materials:

small shoeboxes	Playmobile™ or Fisher-Price™ animals:
pop-up tissue boxes	horses, goats, chickens, etc.
old-fashioned clothespins	fabric scraps
spring-type clothespins	yarn
construction paper	white glue and hot glue
clay	tuna can
books about Bible Times	small rocks
books on model design	paint

Note: Before beginning, look at pictures of life in ancient times. Notice how houses were designed with patio-rooftops, stairs up the side, and round-topped windows. Find a picture of a marketplace, and learn what is sold there. Learn about the occupations of the villagers.

Set-up Location: Use a hearth, coffee table, or top of a low bookshelf to display the village. Students like to work with their village, so keep it within their reach.

Houses: Cut windows and doors in small boxes. Pop-up tissue boxes are perfect. Strips of cardboard may be hot glued around the top edges of the houses, forming a roof top patio. Stairs may be made from cardboard strips folded accordion style and hot glued to the side of a house. Save some boxes for market stalls. Houses may be spray painted. Spray paint will stick to glossy boxes better than tempera.

Trees: Use dowel rods cut in 12" lengths and stained brown or left plain. Cut out several feather shapes of green construction paper. Children may snip the edges of the feather shapes to look like palm fronds. Push a thumb tack through four or five "palm fronds," then into the end of the dowel rod. A small hammer helps.

Villagers: Craft stores sell old-fashioned clothespins that are prepared for doll-making. They come with wooden stands as well. Or use old-fashioned clothespins and stand them in a lump of clay. Prepare as follows.

Drill a small hole through the "shoulders" of several old-fashioned clothespins (the kind without a spring). Saw off the rounded "feet." Push a pipe cleaner through the drilled hole, creating two arms. Cut to desired length, and bend "hands" back. Dress the dolls in striped or solid fabrics. Try cotton, drapery scraps, burlap, and seersucker. A simple elongated rectangle with a tiny hole in the center makes an easy tunic that slips over the doll's head. Tie at the waist with yarn. Draw a face with permanent marker, and glue yarn bits for hair. Try braids or long hair on women dolls, and add a head covering. For very short fuzzy hair, snip yarn into a pile of fuzzy bits, smear glue on doll head, then roll head in fuzz. Press gently onto head with fingertip.

Dress some rich villagers and some poor villagers. Use black crayon to "smudge" clothing. Get creative with your villagers and visitors. Create family members, traders, shepherds, Pharoah, Egyptians, Hebrew warriors, as well as specific characters from your lessons.

Market Place: Read about the role of the marketplace in ancient times. It was a place of buying and selling, and getting the latest news. Use pop-top tissue boxes or other small boxes. Cut three sides out completely, leaving a back and two front "posts." Children enjoy making market items from clay or Sculpey™. Make baskets of clay (or use tiny dollhouse ones) and fill them with tiny clay fruits and vegetables. Roll up 3" x 4" pieces of fabric and tie with yarn for the weaver to sell. Make a money changer's table from a jewelry box, using gold Lego™ coins (or paper punched yellow paper) for his cash. Awnings of construction paper may be cut and glued along the fronts of the stalls and held up with popsicle sticks stuck in clay.

Camel Caravan: Cut several camel body shapes from construction paper. Draw features with marker or crayon. Clamp on two clothespins (the kind with springs) per camel for legs. Clothespins may be stained brown with watercolor or very watery tempera. Staple yarn loops for reins. Stand these in a row just outside the village with a trader or two.

Village Well: Hot glue small rocks around the sides of a tuna can. Set this near the center of the village. Make some clay water pots and place them near the well. Place toy animals near the well, and a boy to watch over them, staff in hand.

Set up the village and have fun acting out Bible stories and daily village life. Guests to your home will surely want a tour!

Teacher's Note: *Remember that for most students, **the learning is in the doing**. Enthusiasm is highest while the village is being constructed. The village houses and dolls may be packed up and displayed in the future.*

Make a Model Tabernacle

**Making this model will help your students visualize the tabernacle
God designed. Only as they try to duplicate it from Scripture
will they realize how awe-inspiring it must have been.**

Focus: Students create a simple replica of the Tabernacle from Scripture references.

Materials: cardboard base 42" x 22"
white glue or spray adhesive, hot glue
construction paper in white, gray, red, and tan
copies of tabernacle patterns (use card stock)
white tissue paper, markers
sand

Introduction: God placed a great deal of importance on the Tabernacle. Only two chapters in the Bible are devoted to the Creation of the universe, but nearly forty-five chapters in Exodus, Leviticus, and Numbers are used to describe the building of the Tabernacle. It was a symbol of his dwelling with Israel.
Like any tent, the Tabernacle was designed to be taken apart and moved. The children of Israel brought offerings for the building: fine linen, animal skins, gold, silver, brass, and precious stones. Many artisans devoted their skills to its construction. God gave very specific instructions that had to be followed precisely.

Construction: This model Tabernacle is a simplified version of the beautifully intricate one described in Scripture. It is close to scale, but can only begin to imitate the grandeur of the original. Encourage those who are interested to pursue this study and add to what is provided here.

> **Cardboard base (42" x 22"):** Use a marker to label compass directions on the base. The two long sides are north and south; the short ends are east and west. Spray base with spray adhesive, or coat with a water-glue mixture. Sprinkle sand all over base, without covering direction labels. Shake off excess.
>
> **Building:** Cut out the tabernacle wall pieces and glue tabs to form a rectangular building. As beautiful as the tabernacle was, the floor was desert sand. Set the "walls" on the sandy base so that the tabernacle back is about 4 inches from the west end. Assemble the outer tent in the same way and attach to the outer edge of the base. Hot glue may be helpful.

Furnishings: Use the patterns provided to make the furniture. Photocopy them onto card stock if possible and assemble. Use the veil provided, or cut a rectangle of tissue paper that will fit across the tabernacle as a divider between the Holy Place and the Holy of Holies. Cut it 1/2" wider than the width of the tabernacle. Fold 1/4" back on each end as a tab. Use colored pencils or fine markers to draw designs like in the Tabernacle Patterns. These represent the beautiful embroidery described in Exodus 26:31. Carefully glue tabs of veil to inside of tabernacle, about 4 1/8" from the tabernacle back. This end of the tabernacle is the Holy of Holies, and the rest of the tabernacle is the Holy Place. Arrange the tabernacle furniture in the tabernacle according to diagram below. (Optional: Spray paint the furniture gold.)

Coverings: Over the top of the Tabernacle were four coverings. The first covering could be seen from the inside of the Tabernacle and was made of linen. Intricate embroidery in red, blue and purple was worked by many hands. Cut a piece of white construction paper the length of the tabernacle and long enough to reach the ground on one side and down to the ground on the other side. Use this piece as a pattern and cut the gray, red and tan construction paper the same size. Decorate the white "linen" covering with your red, blue and purple marker. Place it over the Tabernacle.

The second covering was made of goats hair. Fold and place the gray covering over the Tabernacle.

The third covering was made of ram skins dyed red. Fold and place the red covering over the Tabernacle.

The fourth covering was of badger skin. Fold and place the tan covering over the Tabernacle.

When the Tabernacle model is finished, read Exodus 40:17-38. Imagine the excitement as all Israel watched this huge monument to God's holiness be raised.

See Numbers 4 for information about how the tabernacle was to be moved.

Fascinating Fact: The Holy of Holies was a perfect cube.

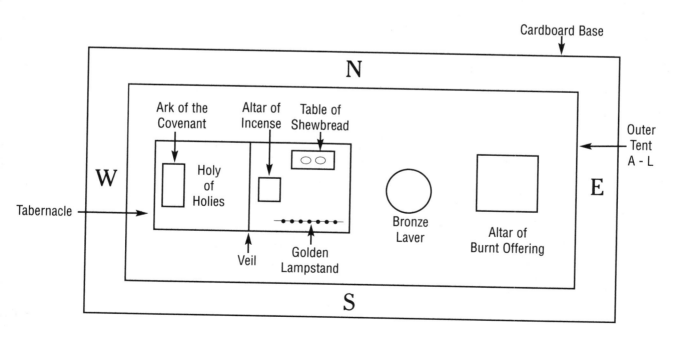

The tabernacle is drawn a bit oversized so the position of the furniture may be easily understood.

Tabernacle Patterns

Cut on solid lines - fold on dashed lines

[Glue to Tabernacle C]

B

Tabernacle
B

[Tabernacle End]

A

Tabernacle
A

Cut on solid lines - fold on dashed lines

[Glue left side of Tabernacle Front here]

C

Tabernacle
C

**Cut on solid lines -
fold on dashed lines**

[Glue to Tabernacle A]

D

Tabernacle
D

**Cut on solid lines -
fold on dashed lines**

Tabernacle Front

[Glue to Tabernacle D]

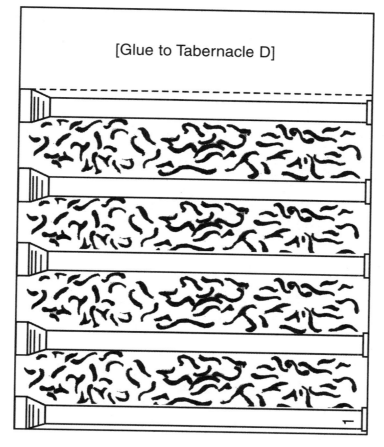

Veil

**Cut on solid lines -
fold on dashed lines**

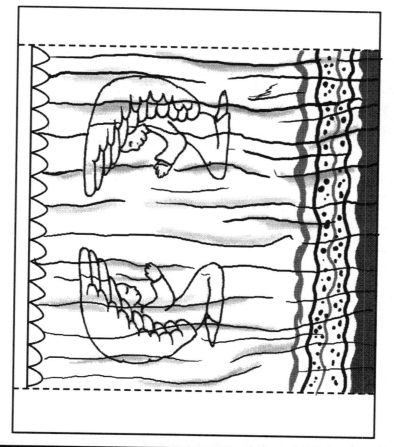

Furniture

Candlestick Diagram

Candlestick

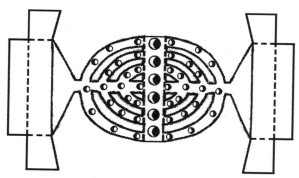

Fold and glue candlestick as in Candlestick Diagram

Laver Diagram

Laver

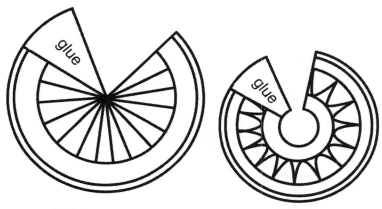

Fold and glue Laver as in Laver Diagram

Table of Shewbread

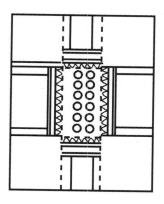

Ark of Covenant

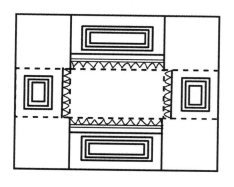

Cut on solid lines - fold on dashed lines

Altar of Burnt Offering

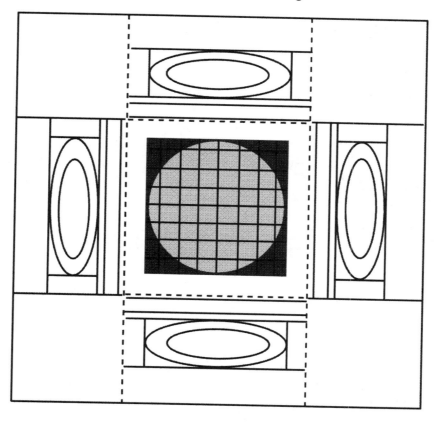

Cherubim Diagram

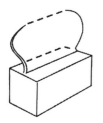

Cherubim

[Fold and glue cherubim
to Ark of Covenant
as in sketch above]

Altar of Incense

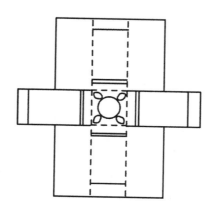

High Priest

Cut on solid lines - fold on dashed lines

Outer Tent A

[Glue to B]

Outer Tent B

[Glue to C]

Outer Tent C

[Glue to D]

Cut on solid lines - fold on dashed lines

Outer Tent D

[Glue to E]

Outer Tent E

[Glue to F]

Outer Tent F

[Glue to G]

Cut on solid lines - fold on dashed lines

Outer Tent G

[Glue to H]

G

Outer Tent L

[Glue to A]

L

Outer Tent K

[Glue to L]

K

Cut on solid lines - fold on dashed lines

81

Outer Tent J

[Glue to K]

Outer Tent I

[Glue to J]

Outer Tent H

[Glue to I]

Cut on solid lines - fold on dashed lines

Tabernacle Top - Part 1

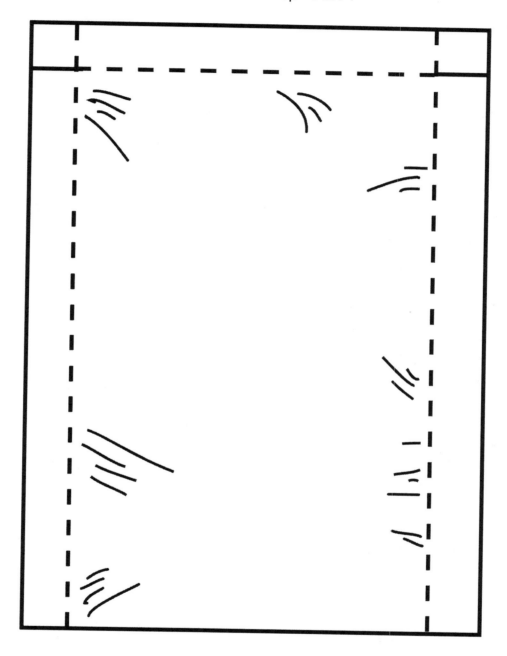

Cut on solid lines - fold on dashed lines

Tabernacle Top - Part 2

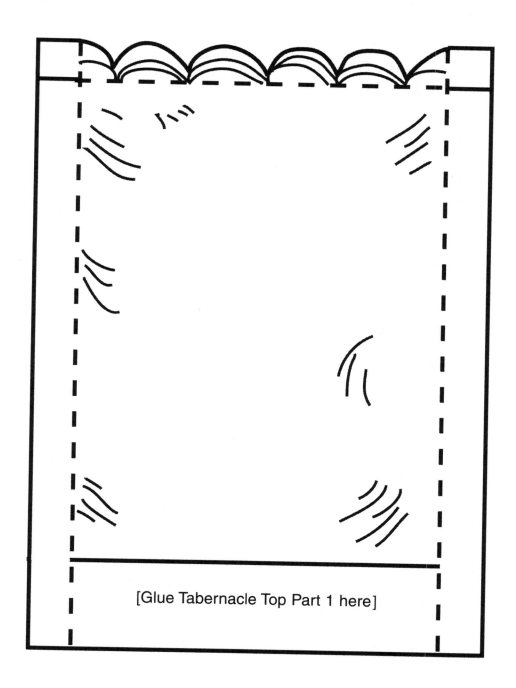

[Glue Tabernacle Top Part 1 here]

Cut on solid lines - fold on dashed lines

Pillars of History, Part I

Keys to the Past

Each *Keys to the Past* is made up of 16 inside pages, plus a front and back cover. All the covers to the *Keys to the Past* are located at the front of this section. These may be photocopied on colored paper. The covers are followed by the inside pages of the books.

How to Photocopy the *Keys to the Past*

Note: These pages are easier to photocopy if they are taken out of the book. The *Keys to the Past* are provided as consumable pages which may be cut out of the *Pillars of History* book at the line on the top of each page. If, however, you wish to make photocopies for your students, you can do so by following the instructions below.

Be sure to try one book before you copy the entire set. To photocopy the inside pages of the *Keys to the Past*:

1. Note that there is a "Star" above the line at the top of each *Key* sheet.

2. Locate the *Key* side that has a Star on it above page 16. Position this sheet on the glass of your photocopier so the side of the sheet which contains page 16 is facing down, and the Star above page 16 is in the left corner closest to you. Photocopy the page.

3. Turn the *Key* sheet over so that the side of the *Key* sheet containing page 6 is now face down. Position the sheet so the Star above page 6 is again in the left corner closest to you.

4. Insert the previously photocopied paper into the copier again, inserting it face down, with the Star at the end of the sheet that enters the copier last. Photocopy the page. (Some copiers may require you to insert the previously photocopied paper face up.)

5. Repeat steps 1 through 4, above, for each *Key* sheet.

To photocopy the covers of the *Keys to the Past Books:*

1. Insert "Cover Sheet A" in the photocopier with a Star positioned in the left corner closest to you, facing down. Photocopy the page.

2. Turn "Cover Sheet A" over so that the side you just photocopied is now facing you. Position the sheet so the Star is again in the left corner closest to you, facing down.

3. Insert the previously photocopied paper into the copier again, inserting it face down, with the Star entering the copier last. Photocopy the page.

4. Repeat steps 1 through 3, above, for "Cover Sheets" B, C, D, E, and F.

Note: The owner of this book has permission to photocopy the *Keys to the Past Book* pages and covers for classroom use only.

How to assemble the *Keys to the Past*

Once you have made the photocopies or cut the consumable pages out of this book, you are ready to assemble your *Keys to the Past*. To do so, follow these instructions:

1. Cut each sheet, both covers and inside pages, on the solid lines.

2. Lay the inside pages on top of one another in this order: pages 2 and 15, pages 4 and 13, pages 6 and 11, pages 8 and 9.

3. Fold the stacked pages on the dotted line, with pages 8 and 9 facing each other.

4. Turn the pages over so that pages 1 and 16 are on top.

5. Place the appropriate cover pages on top of the inside pages, with the front cover facing up.

6. Staple on the dotted line in two places.

You now have completed *Keys to the Past.*

Seasons of the Year

Keys to the Past #4

Ancient Architecture

Keys to the Past #3

How the Torah Came to Us

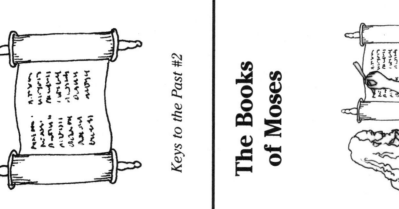

Keys to the Past #2

The Books of Moses

Keys to the Past #1

PILLARS OF THE HEBREW NATION

Travel and Trade

Keys to the Past #6

PILLARS OF THE HEBREW NATION

Egyptian gods

Keys to the Past #8

PILLARS OF THE HEBREW NATION

Nomadic Life

Keys to the Past #5

PILLARS OF THE HEBREW NATION

Ancient Hebrew Clothing

Keys to the Past #7

History Books

Keys to the Past #12

A Woman's Life

Keys to the Past #11

PILLARS OF THE HEBREW NATION

PILLARS OF THE HEBREW NATION

Hebrew Feasts of the Lord

Keys to the Past #10

Ancient Hebrew Food

Keys to the Past #9

PILLARS OF THE HEBREW NATION

PILLARS OF THE HEBREW NATION

The book of Genesis explains the creation of the universe. It reveals God's relationship to human beings.

5

Genesis reports God's choice of one man. This man was Abraham. The rest of the Old Testament is the story of Abraham's family.

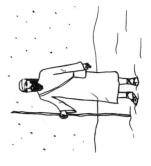

7

The book of Numbers tells about the Hebrew people and their rebellion toward God. Because of their rebellion, God did not allow them to enter Canaan for 40 years. Chapter 1 and Chapter 26 record the numbering of the Hebrews.

Exodus means "to go out." It tells the story of Moses leading the Hebrews out of Egypt and describes how God cared for them in the desert, even though they complained.

The Hebrew people call the first five books of the Old Testament the "books of Moses" because they were written by him.

They are also called the Pentateuch, which means "Five Books" in Greek.

Moses wrote the books in a different order than they appear in the Scriptures. He wrote all the books in Hebrew.

Genesis   1400 B.C.
Exodus   1440 B.C.
Numbers   1406 B.C.
Deuteronomy   1406 B.C.
Leviticus   1446 B.C.

Fascinating Facts

The "Books of Moses" does not contain the oldest books in the Bible. Job is actually much older, being written around 2000 B.C.

Deuteronomy is filled with Moses' sermons reviewing God's law. He reminds the new generation of the journey God brought them through and what God expects of them.

Unlike pagan cultures, Genesis teaches the worship of one true God. It explains the origin of sin. It also tells the story of a worldwide flood.

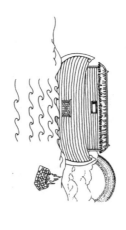

Leviticus is a book of laws for holy living. It was written at Mt. Sinai to teach the Levite priests how to perform the feasts and sacrifices to the Lord.

Moses was Hebrew but grew up as a privileged Egyptian, educated in the Scriptures under the finest teachers.

Did You Know?

Most of the miracles in the Scriptures took place during two short periods of time. The first was during Moses' life and the second during Elijah and Elisha's lives.

Abraham's family became the Hebrew people or Israelites. Today they are called Jews and live all over the world.

In Exodus, Abraham's descendants are enslaved in Egypt. The stories show God's power as He sent plagues to the Egyptians and to Pharoah.

His work was translated to Greek in about 250 B.C. Some Greek-speaking Jews living in Egypt asked the Pharoah for help. He paid the expenses for seventy scholars to make a Greek translation of the Hebrew Books.

At the second numbering of the Hebrews, all those who had lived in Egypt were dead. Their children were ready to enter Canaan.

Canaan

It is so old that it is hard to know how the writings were collected. We know that from early times people have written important things and kept the writings in a special place.

It may be that the stories were preserved by storytellers who handed them down from generation to generation. Later Moses may have written these down.

Moses and others would have taken great care of these sacred writings. The scrolls were gathered together with other writings between 622 B.C. and 100 A.D.

Sheets of papyrus were beaten into long strips and rolled up into scrolls. These were the earliest "books."

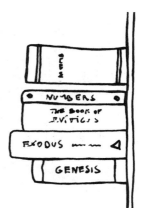

The Hebrew Scripture is a special book. God Himself inspired men to write His message to the Hebrew people.

The Books of Moses make up the "Torah." Torah is the Hebrew word for "law," but it also means "guidance" and "instruction."

NUMBERS
THE BOOK OF LEVITICUS
EXODUS
GENESIS

Fascinating Facts

The early Hebrew alphabet had 22 letters, but no vowels. Later, a system of dots was invented to represent vowels.

Deuteronomy 11:18-19 says: "Remember these commands and cherish them. Tie them on your arms and wear them on your foreheads..." Some Jews today still wear bits of the Torah in small leather boxes on their arms and foreheads.

6

Jewish tradition is that Moses wrote the Torah. However, the stories in Genesis happened before Moses was born. Did God inspire Moses to write these? Did the people in the stories record and preserve their own writings?

8

Moses would have used scrolls to record the history of the Hebrews and the Laws of God. In fact, God told Moses to "write this on a scroll as something to be remembered..."

11

In Israel, animal skins were turned into a very thin type of leather that could be used for writing. This material is called vellum. Rectangles of vellum were stitched together and rolled into scrolls.

9

Moses grew up in the palace of the Pharoah and was well educated. He learned to write on papyrus, a paper made from the papyrus plant.

2

The Old Testament contains 39 very different books. These books span 1500 years. They record the history of a nation of people who have been called Hebrews, Israelites, and Jews.

15

Did You Know?

In 622 B.C., young King Josiah of Judah found a copy of the Torah in the temple and realized its importance. The High Priest read the entire Torah to the people of Israel. The people once more obeyed God's Law.

4

The Torah is written in Hebrew because that is the language the descendants of Abraham spoke.

13

The Jewish people worldwide still read the Torah when they gather in synagogues. The huge scrolls are treated with great respect and kept in a special box called an "ark."

Lines of holes show where posts once stood. Depth and width of a foundation shows how tall a wall might have been. Archaeologists dig carefully to avoid damaging old buildings.

One of the oldest cities known is Jericho. It may have been established as early as 8000 B.C. People who study the site have found city upon city there, indicating it has been rebuilt repeatedly. (Joshua 6:26)

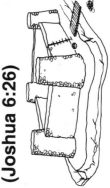

Some of the most famous buildings in the world are very old. The pyramids in Egypt date from 2565 B.C. Thousands of workers labored many years to construct them.

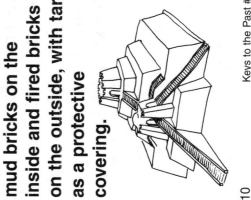

Keys to the Past #3

12

About the same time, a ziggurat was built in Iraq. It was built of mud bricks on the inside and fired bricks on the outside, with tar as a protective covering.

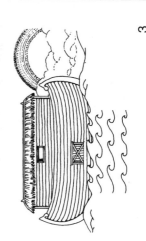

Keys to the Past #3

10

What we know about ancient buildings comes from archaeologists who look for clues. Clues are found in pottery, art, and ancient texts. Some clues are hidden in the ground.

Keys to the Past #3

1

Noah's building project saved his life and the lives of his family. God gave Noah the instructions to build the ark. Noah built it exactly as God told him.

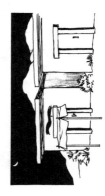

Keys to the Past #3

3

Fascinating Facts

Iron tools were hard and used when working with stone. Tools made of bronze were softer and used on wood.

Keys to the Past #3

16

Early people in many places built their homes of mud bricks dried in the sun. These homes were cool in summer, warm in winter, easy to repair and inexpensive to build.

Keys to the Past #3

14

Archaeologists learn how skilled people worked with wood and stone; how they lived and how they worshipped. These clues give us information about workers in a community.

Magnificent palaces dating from 2500 B.C. have been found on the island of Crete. The palaces were two or more levels high and had efficient drains and plumbing.

In Genesis 4:17, we read about Cain building a city. He named it after his son, Enoch. Since Cain's farming ability was cursed by God, opening a trade center was a way for him to make a living.

Did You Know?

Early carpenters had primitive forms of the same tools available today: drill and bits, hammer, mallet, chisel, ruler and compass, plane, nails, ax, adze, saw, square, awl and plumb line.

Another ancient settlement is Catal Huyuk. Its houses were one story high and had door-holes in the roof. Ladders leading to the roof were pulled in when enemies came to the town.

Remains of a town from 2500 B.C. were found in Pakistan. The town was well planned, with streets and drainage systems laid in straight lines. Many of the houses were identical.

Many cultures designed and built elaborate buildings and towns. Archaeologists and architects work together to understand building structures.

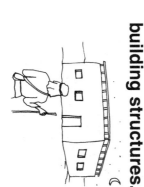

Using ramps and levers, men succeeded in stacking huge stone bricks as high as 148 meters. Finished pyramids were encased in white limestone.

The rains poured into dry stream beds. Temporary flooding was caused by sudden downpours. The rains brought a beautiful, green countryside.

5

Winter was the time to plant vegetables: lentils, onions, leeks, garlic, and cucumbers. These would be ready to harvest by the summer.

7

Grain had to be separated from the stalks. It was beaten with rods or trampled by oxen. This process was called "threshing."

Keys to the Past #4

12

A hot, dry, dusty wind blew from the south. The plants turned brown. Grain planted in late fall was ready to be harvested.

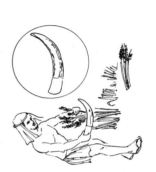

Keys to the Past #4

10

The seasons of the year were the rhythm of life for the Hebrew people. Once settled in Canaan, they found each season had its own work.

Keys to the Past #4

1

Early autumn brought the harvest of olives and grapes. Mid-October was the time of the early rains, sometimes called the "former" rains.

Keys to the Past #4

3

Fascinating Facts

Almost every 20 years snow falls in hilltop Jerusalem. Sometimes it falls in the lowlands.

Keys to the Past #4

16

Farmers did not need fertilizers for the rich soil. Instead they followed God's law and allowed their farms, vineyards, and orchards to rest one season out of seven.

Keys to the Past #4

14

8

grew
quickly.

crops and
wildflowers

harvested. The

citrus fruits were

trees blossomed, and

"latter" rains. Almond

rain falling after April.

heavy rains called the

With spring came

9

Once the rains began,
people plowed their
fields and planted
wheat, barley, and flax.
They planted in rows
or scattered seed
haphazardly.

4

6

The temperature
dropped with the
arrival of winter. Frost
might be seen, but
rarely snow. December
and January were cool
and rainy.

Farmers used a sickle
to harvest the wheat.
Early sickles were
made of a stone called
flint. Later, sickles
were made of metal.

11

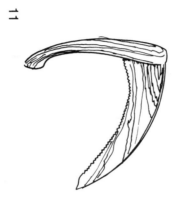

Summer signaled the
dry season with little

Migrating eagles and
storks from Africa
were seen on their way
to Europe.

2

In that day sowing seeds
was done as described
in the parable. It was
done in accordance to
the seasons which were
incorporated into 12
months as described in
this rhyme:

*2 months of olive harvest, then 2 months for
sowing grain, 2 months to sow the later seeds
all through the winter rain. 1 month to hoe
the flax and leave it drying in the sun. 1
month to gather barley now the harvest has
begun. 1 month to gather sheaves of wheat
and feast with joy and mirth. 2 months to
tend the grapevines that give wine to all the
earth. 1 month to gather summer fruits that
ripen in the heat.*

Did You Know?

Most of the land of
Israel has mild winters
and warm summers
with 35 cm of rain a
year. Crops grow well
there.

15

Fruits were gathered.
Pomegranates, figs,
and grapes ripened
one after another.
Some fruits were
preserved by drying
them in the sun.

13

The animals provided almost everything their owners needed. Camels and donkeys could carry riders or possessions.

The nomads used animal skins and wool to make shoes and clothes. Clothing colors were the same as the sheep: white, gray, brown, and black. Even the tents were made of woven goat hair.

Abraham's grandson, Jacob, became rich living the nomadic life. He increased both his father-in-law's herd and his own.

When they settled in Canaan, both Abraham and Lot had large flocks needing pastureland. Their herdsmen began to fight over water and land.

Many people in ancient lands were nomads. This means they travelled from place to place with their flocks and herds.

Nomadic people needed to travel to find new pastures for their animals. Animals grazing too long in one place can damage the land.

Fascinating Facts

Goat hair is naturally waterproof and tough enough to stand up to scorching desert heat and wind.

Joseph's brothers wanted to get rid of him. They had no trouble selling him because merchants travelled in caravans along trade routes among nomadic people.

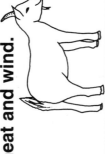

Cattle, goats, and sheep provided meat for food. Milk was used for drinking, cheese-making, and yogurt.

Keys to the Past #5

6

When more than one nomadic tribe settled in an area, there were sometimes arguments over pastureland and water.

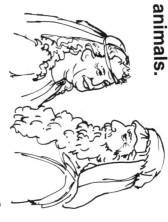

Keys to the Past #5

8

They needed to live separately. Abraham gave Lot first choice of land. Lot chose the green pastures near the towns of Sodom and Gomorrah.

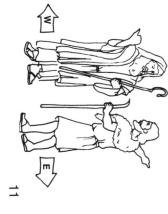

11

Abraham became a nomad when he left Ur to obey God. He traveled with his wife, Sarah, his nephew, Lot, and many servants and animals.

9

Wealth was measured by the number of animals owned by a man. A man with large numbers of cattle, goats, donkeys, camels, and sheep was a wealthy man.

Keys to the Past #5

4

They lived in tents that could easily be taken down when it was time to travel. The tents were warm in cold weather and could be opened to catch the breeze in hot weather.

Keys to the Past #5

2

Did You Know?

Nomads today still live much the same way people did in Abraham's day; living off the land and depending on their animals.

15

Many years later, Jacob was living in Canaan with his twelve sons. He sent his son Joseph to check on his brothers, who had found pastureland some distance away.

13

Travelers could hire a light two-wheeled cart at the town gate to travel to the next town. Heavy four-wheeled wagons could be hired to carry large loads, but they had to travel slowly because of the bumpy road.

Horses weren't used often. They were expensive to buy and uncomfortable to ride because saddles had not been invented yet.

Caravans traveled to India, China, and Africa for spices, medicines, ivory, cotton, and silks. They brought olive oil and wine from Italy, and grain from Egypt.

Keys to the Past #6

12

Merchants traveled in caravans, moving across vast stretches of desert along established trade routes. A caravan leader organized the men and camels into "relays" that relieved each other at certain points.

Keys to the Past #6

10

In ancient times, roads were not much more than paths. They were filled with brambles, weeds, rocks, and ruts. Most people traveled on foot or by donkey.

1

Keys to the Past #6

Camping out along the road at night was very dangerous unless the group of travelers was large. It was safer to stay at an inn.

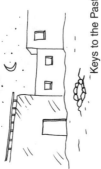

3

Keys to the Past #6

Did You Know?

Caravans stopped at "caravansaries" to shelter for the night. They rested and watered their animals. Here the merchants told stories and passed along news.

16

Keys to the Past #6

The empty ships loaded up with balsam from Palestine, cedar from Lebanon, and purple dye from Tyre. They sailed to Africa and Egypt to complete the cycle.

14

Keys to the Past #6

6

Donkeys were sure-footed on rocky roads and in the hills. They could carry heavy loads. Traveling 20 miles in a day, donkeys were ideal for personal travel or for traders.

Keys to the Past #6

8

Camels could carry 400 pounds of goods and travel 14 days without water. They could travel in wind storms and on blistering sand. They were used for personal travel and caravan trade.

Keys to the Past #6

11

From Arabia came frankincense and myrrh. From Asia Minor came fine rugs and embroideries. Bitumen, a kind of tar, came from Mesopotamia.

9

Merchants traveled far to buy and sell the goods people wanted. They displayed their wares at city gates or in market stalls.

2

Thieves hid along the roadside, making travel by foot dangerous. Most people only traveled when necessary.

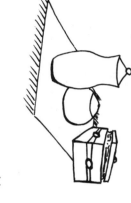

Keys to the Past #6

4

Few inns were clean and inviting. Most were dirty, had bedbugs and no bathroom. Travelers provided their own meals, sleeping mats, and oil lamps. Staying with a friend was more pleasant.

Keys to the Past #6

Did You Know?

13

Merchants used beam balances to weigh their goods. Local officials checked these for accuracy to make sure prices were fair.

15

Some of these items came on ships. The goods were loaded onto caravans which took them to towns and villages.

Camel and goat hair were spun into thread and woven into a sturdy heavy cloth for outerwear and tents.

5

Women spent many hours making cloth. Very rarely did they have any extra to sell. Only the wealthy had more than one or two sets of clothing.

7

God's law said that if a man gave his cloak as a pledge, it was to be returned to him at night. This is because his cloak was his only covering. Exodus 22:26-27.

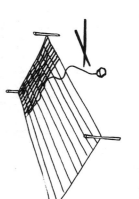

Keys to the Past #7

12

A soldier or shepherd wore a leather girdle providing a place to hang his weapons and tools.

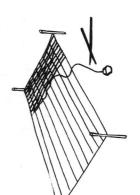

Keys to the Past #7

10

In Hebrew times, women made clothing from materials gathered from animals and plants.

Keys to the Past #7

1

Wool was then combed to untangle the fibers. It was spun into thread and woven into cloth.

3

Fascinating Facts

Aaron's High Priest clothing was of red, blue, and scarlet linen. His gold breastplate was studded with 12 precious stones representing the 12 tribes of Israel.

Keys to the Past #7

16

Jewelry was made of precious stones, ivory, gold, silver, or shells. Earrings, nose rings, necklaces, bracelets, and pendants were worn on special occasions.

Keys to the Past #7

14

The blue-flowering flax plant was grown to make linen. The stalks were dried, then soaked in water to make a beautiful soft cloth. Priests dressed in linen.

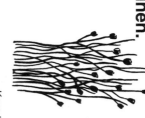

Cloaks were worn in chilly weather. They were like tunics with sleeves and an open front. A cloak made a blanket at night, could be folded into a bag to carry things, or fashioned into a baby carrier.

People wore a basic tunic that reached to the knee or ankle. These were made from rectangles of cloth with a slit in the center. This style did not waste any of the precious hand-woven cloth.

A girdle was a belt made of leather or cloth worn at the waist. The folds of a cloth girdle were used as pockets for coins and other items.

Wool was a favorite material. Sheep were sheared once a year, and the wool was washed by a person called a "fuller." This was a smelly process and took place far from the homes.

The finished cloth was the same color as sheep, ranging from shades of white to shades of brown. Dyes of red, blue and purple were expensive, especially purple. Only kings could afford purple clothes.

Did You Know?

In Bible times, sometimes men needed a way to seal a business agreement. To show his trustworthiness, one man would pull off his shoe and give it to the other man.

Most people went barefoot or wore sandals. Sandals were made of leather with a sole made of wood or palm-tree bark.

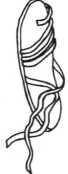

Because Pharoah would not let the Israelites leave Egypt, God wanted to show Pharoah He was more powerful than any Egyptian god.

5

Heqet was their goddess of childbirth or fertility and was worshiped in the form of a frog. So God sent frogs to bother the Egyptians.

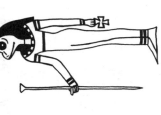

7

Osiris was their god of crops and harvest. God mocked him with a plague of locusts that ate every plant in sight.

Keys to the Past #8

12

Hathor was their goddess of love, protection, and beauty and was represented by a cow. She could not protect the cattle when God sent death to them during the fifth plague.

Keys to the Past #8

10

In Hebrew times, Egypt was a powerful nation. The Egyptians were fine horsemen and went to battle in chariots. They built huge temples and produced great works of art.

Keys to the Past #8

1

The Egyptians believed the gods could answer prayers and work miracles. Worshiping the gods was part of daily life.

3

Fascinating Facts

Priests made offerings to the gods every day. The priests offered food to their gods and dressed them each morning.

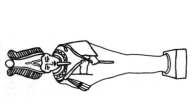

Keys to the Past #8

16

Tawaret and Bes were the protectors of homes and babies to the Egyptians. When God took the life of every firstborn, these gods were powerless to stop Him.

Keys to the Past #8

14

6

The first plague, when the Nile turned to blood, mocked Sobek, their god of water, and Khnum, controller-god of the Nile.

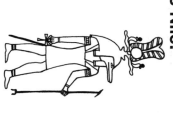

8

Set was their god of desert storms and chaos. With the third plague, God had Moses strike the sand, and "the dust of the sand became lice."

11

Isis was their goddess of healing. God mocked her with the sixth plague of boils. Their sky goddess, Nut, was insulted when God sent giant hail that killed men, animals, and broke trees.

9

With the fourth plague, when God sent a plague of flies and insects, the Egyptians may have wondered why they worshiped beetles.

2

The Egyptian people worshiped their Pharoah, or king, as though he were a god. They also worshiped cats, frogs, and other animals. They even worshiped their river.

4

The temples built for their gods were private. Only priests, kings, and queens could enter. The common people could not worship in the temples.

15

None of the Egyptian's gods could help them when the one true God sent plagues. The Egyptians and Pharoah began to realize Moses' God was more powerful than their gods.

Did You Know?

13

The Egyptians' most important god was Ra, sun god and creator of the world. He had the head of a bird and a hat like the sun. God sent the plague of darkness to mock Ra.

Cooks made thick soups with beans, peas, and lentils. They used salt, onions, cumin, garlic, and leeks to flavor their dishes.

5

Grains were ground for use in breads and cakes or boiled for cereal. Barley was the most commonly used grain.

7

Mothers sometimes sent a "sack lunch" with her children when they left for the day. The lunch may have included two hollow loaves of bread filled with olives and cheese.

Keys to the Past #9

12

For dessert, the family might enjoy dried figs boiled in grape molasses, honeycomb, honey "donuts," locust biscuits, or fig and cinnamon cakes.

Keys to the Past #9

10

Most people in Bible times ate only two meals a day. Breakfast was bread, dried fruit and cheese. It was eaten on the way to the workplace or fields.

1

Keys to the Past #9

Wild birds such as dove or quail were stewed in gravy with rice or other grains. Salted or dried fish was served with herbs.

3

Fascinating Facts

Utensils were not very common. Two people shared a bowl and ate with their fingers or scooped the food with bread.

Keys to the Past #9

16

In town, drinking water was sold on the street in goatskins. Fruit and vegetables could be bought fresh at the market as often as needed.

Keys to the Past #9

14

Both leavened and unleavened bread were served. Leavened bread had yeast or sourdough bacteria in it; unleavened bread did not. It was like matzah.

6

Keys to the Past #9

The Canaan climate was ideal for growing many fruits: grapes, figs, olives, mulberries, pomegranites, apricots, plums, oranges, lemons, melons, dates, almonds, and walnuts.

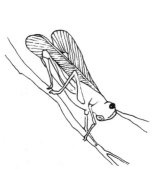

8

Keys to the Past #9

People drank water, red wine, honey wine, goat's milk, and grape juice.

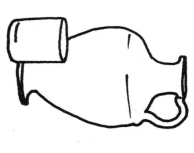

11

Tasty treats included boiled or roasted locusts, fried grasshoppers, and roasted corn.

9

The second meal of the day was the main meal. It was eaten with the family at the end of the work day.

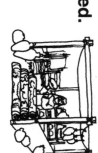

2

Keys to the Past #9

Lamb was sometimes stuffed with vegetables and wrapped in cabbage or grape leaves.

4

Keys to the Past #9

Did You Know?

Since there was no refrigeration, fresh food was dried to keep from spoiling. Drying worked well for fruits and meats. Sometimes meats and fish were dried and salted.

15

Red meat was reserved for special occasions. Jews were not allowed to eat pork, rabbit, or shellfish. These animals were considered "unclean."

13

SHAVUOT

(Also called Pentecost and Day of Firstfruits)

Theme: Revelation and Harvest

When: Seven weeks after Passover

Commemorates: Fire on Mt. Sinai when God gave the Torah.

5

DAYS OF AWE

Theme: Repentance and Restitution

When: Between Rosh Hashana and Yom Kippur

Purpose: Making apologies, righting wrongs, paying debts, seeking to live in awe of God, S'lihot prayers of repentance to God.

7

PURIM

Theme: Deliverance

Season: Late Winter

Food: Haman's Hat Cookies

Commemorates: The story of Esther saving the Jews. Children act out the story by dressing up as characters from the story. Jews today remember the Holocaust.

12

SIMCHAT TORAH

Theme: Rejoicing in God's Word

When: Last day of Sukkot

Purpose: Special readings of the Torah in the synagogue. A time to be thankful that the Jews preserved God's Word.

10

The Feasts of the Lord were given by God to the Jewish people. Some are like a rehearsal for a future prophetic event. Others serve as lessons in God's love for his people.

1

The feasts are like a string of pearls, gracing the year with reflections on who God is and how He cares for His people.

3

Fascinating Facts

Faithful Jews mounted a piece of parchment called a mezuzah on their doorposts. The mezuzah contained a blessing or a bit of God's Word. A person would touch it before entering the house, then kiss his fingertips.

16

Celebrating the Feasts of the Lord help God's people to love God and grow in their faith.

14

ROSH HASHANA
(Jewish New Year)

Theme: Obedience and Provision
Season: Fall
Food: Apple with honey
Commemorates: Abraham's obedience to sacrifice his son and God's provision of the ram to save Isaac.

8

6

HANUKKAH

Theme: Light and Zeal for God's Ways
Season: Winter
Commemorates: Jerusalem was retaken from the Syrians. During that time, a small amount of oil lasted 8 days in the Menorah used in the Temple.

11

SUKKOT
Feast of Tabernacles

Theme: Rejoicing
Season: Fall
Commemorates: Forefathers who camped in the wilderness. Three-sided booths are built with roof branches. People sleep and eat in the booths so they can see the stars above.

9

YOM KIPPUR

Theme: Covering and Forgiveness
Season: Fall
Food: Fasting
Purpose: To think about one's sin and to realize sin needs a blood sacrifice for a covering.

8

The Spring Pilgrimage Festivals are *Passover* and *Shavuot*. The Feasts of the Fall Harvest are *Rosh Hashana, Yom Kippur, Sukkot,* and *Simchat Torah*. The festivals showing God's love are *Hannukah* and *Purim*.

2

PASSOVER

Theme: Redemption
Season: Spring
Commemorates: The sparing of the Hebrew firstborn and the exodus of Israel from Egypt. Different foods are tasted, symbolizing the parts of the story.

15

4

The Feasts of the Lord are thousands of years old. They are celebrated by people all over the world.

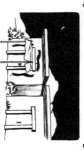

13

Did You Know?

At the end of the Sabbath day, or any holy day, Jews search the sky for three stars in one glance. This means the Holy Day has come to an end.

Only boys went to school, so girls were trained at home in the homemaking arts. Girls learned to spin, weave, sing, dance, and play an instrument.

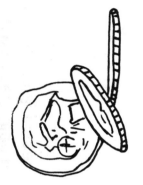

Jewish law required a wife to know which animals were clean and unclean, how to prepare the food, and how to purify and set the table. She also knew how to decorate the home for the Sabbath and special holidays.

In large families, women had their own section of the tent. They were not to mix with the master of the house and his guests, other than to serve them.

12

The amount of the dowry depended on what the bride was worth and how much the groom's family could afford.

10

It was the Hebrew custom for men to be responsible to provide for their wives and daughters. Only the sons received an inheritance.

1

Rebekah left her family to marry Isaac. She showed the same faith Abraham did when he left home in response to God's call.

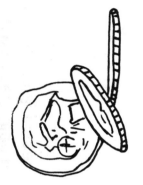

Fascinating Facts

Mothers kept their babies tightly wrapped for the first six months. This was to keep them from thrashing their arms and legs.

16

Some women were gifted midwives. They bathed the newborn in water, rubbed him down with salt to prevent infection, and wrapped him tightly in strips of linen called "swaddling clothes."

14

8

Girls could be betrothed between the ages of 13 and 17. The young men were 17 or 18 years old. The betrothal period lasted a year. The groom gave the girl and her mother gifts.

9

It was the custom for a young man's parents to choose a wife for him. If both families agreed to the match, and if the groom could afford the dowry, or "bride price," then a wedding took place.

4

Women had the important role of managing the home. They prepared meals, cared for animals, wove cloth, made clothes, and gathered the harvest.

15

Women who had no family might become nurse or nanny to the children in a large family. They were respected and loved like a member of the family. When Rebekah left home to marry Isaac, her nurse went with her.

6

Girls learned to be good wives and mothers. They learned how to deliver babies and to treat illnesses with ancient remedies.

11

New brides were worth about 50 shekels. Widows or divorced women were worth only half that amount. Sometimes a groom paid in animals or jewelry. He might pay in service, like Jacob.

2

However, women were not insignificant to God. Some showed remarkable faith and God rewarded them for it.

13

Meanings of names:
Eve: Life
Mary, Miriam: Bitter
Martha: Mistress of the House
Ruth: Something worth seeing
Rebekah: Captivating
Sarai: Princess
Sarah: Queen

Two miraculous battle stories appear in the book of Joshua. The Jericho walls fall down and the sun stands still.

5

Ruth is a love story that took place during the time of the Judges. It shows that God honors those who honor Him, even when their nation does not.

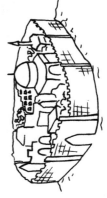

7

I Chronicles is similar to I Samuel in many ways. It reviews the reign of King David, and his accomplishments. It lists genealogies, and establishes the line of David.

12

I and II Kings teach the benefits of obeying God and the dangers of disobeying Him. Due to disobedience, the Hebrew Kingdom split into two parts: Judah and Israel. Israel was taken captive by the Assyrians and later, Judah was taken captive by Babylon.

10

The History Books contain some of the most exciting stories in the Scriptures.

Joshua
Judges
Ruth
I & II Samuel
I & II Kings
I & II Chronicles
Ezra
Nehemiah
Esther

1

I Samuel	1050 B.C.
II Samuel	1010 B.C.
I Kings	970 B.C.
II Kings	586 B.C.
I Chronicles	1003 B.C.
II Chronicles	970 B.C.
Ezra	430 B.C.
Nehemiah.	430 B.C.
Esther.	460 B.C.

3

Fascinating Facts

The book of Joshua mentions the Hittite people. Their existence was confirmed by archaeologists in the nineteenth century. The Hittites descended from Canaan, Noah's grandson.

16

Ezra and Nehemiah wrote most of the books named for them. They tell about the return of the Jews to Jerusalem and the rebuilding of its walls.

14

After Joshua died, God appointed judges to lead his people. The book of Judges tells how the Hebrews turned from God to pagan idolatry. Therefore, God allowed foreign enemies to oppress them.

I Samuel is the story of Israel becoming a nation ruled by kings instead of by God alone. Saul was the first king. David was the second king.

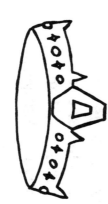

David's reign is described in II Samuel. He was a man after God's own heart. Both his strengths and failures are included in these stories.

I and II Kings include the stories of Elijah and Elisha and the miracles God did through them. These men faithfully rebuked evil kings.

The book of Joshua tells the exciting story of the Hebrew conquest of Canaan. God's people learn to obey, and God gives them victory over the pagan Canaanites.

No one knows for certain who wrote these books. The events took place near the dates given but may have been written down much later.

Joshua	1400 B.C.
Judges	1375 B.C.
Ruth	1375 B.C.

Stories of godly kings may be read in II Chronicles. These stories show that God blessed Judah when they honored him. One godly king was Uzziah who reigned 52 years.

Esther was a Jewish woman who became the Queen of Persia. When the Jews were sentenced to die, she approached the King to plead for their lives.

Graphics Pages

Note: The owner of the book has permission to photocopy the *Graphics Pages* for his/her classroom use only.

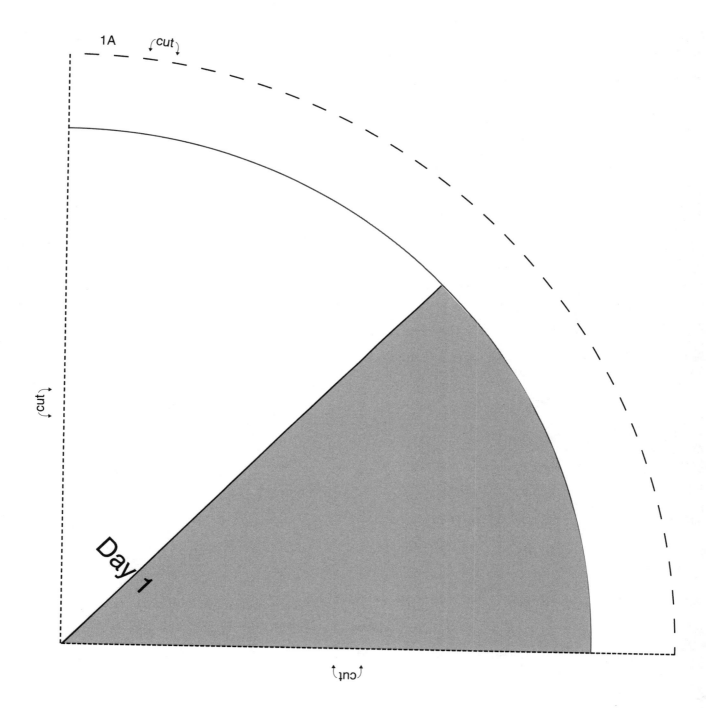

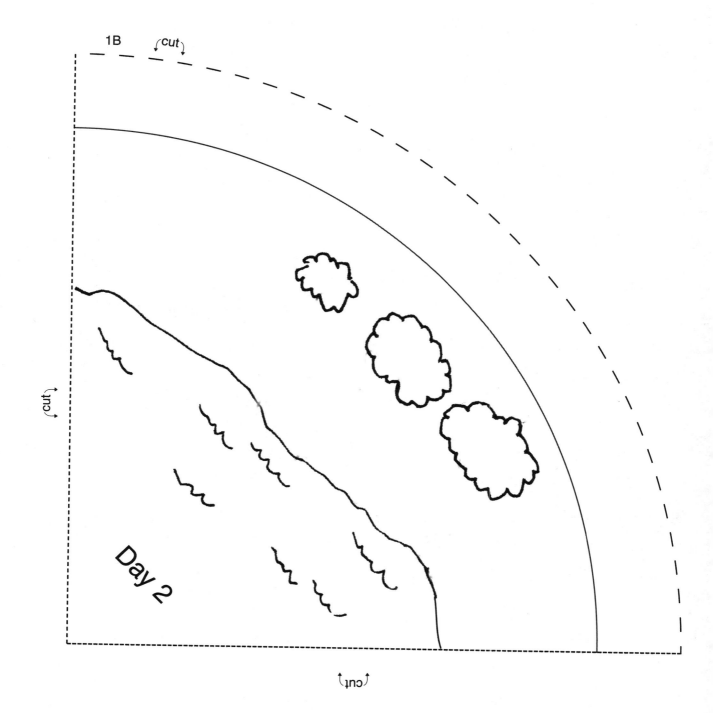

1C   cut

cut

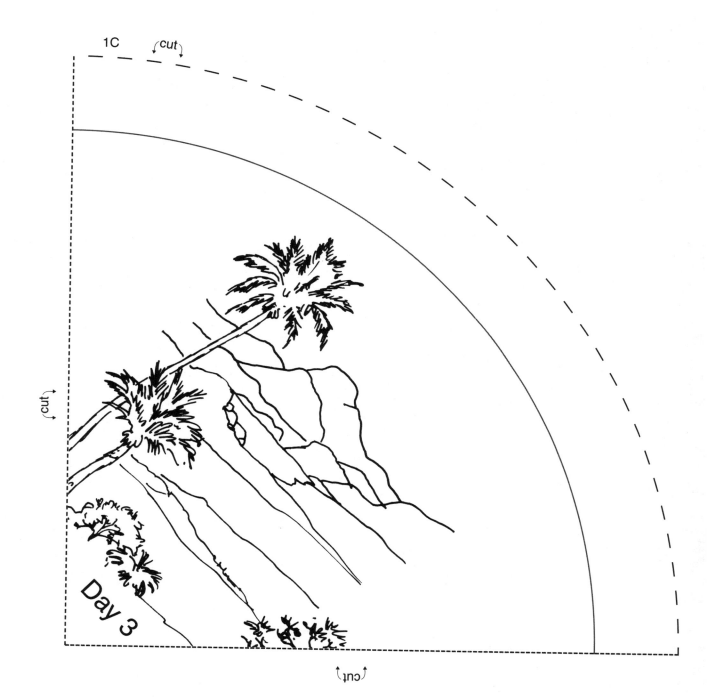

Day 3

cut

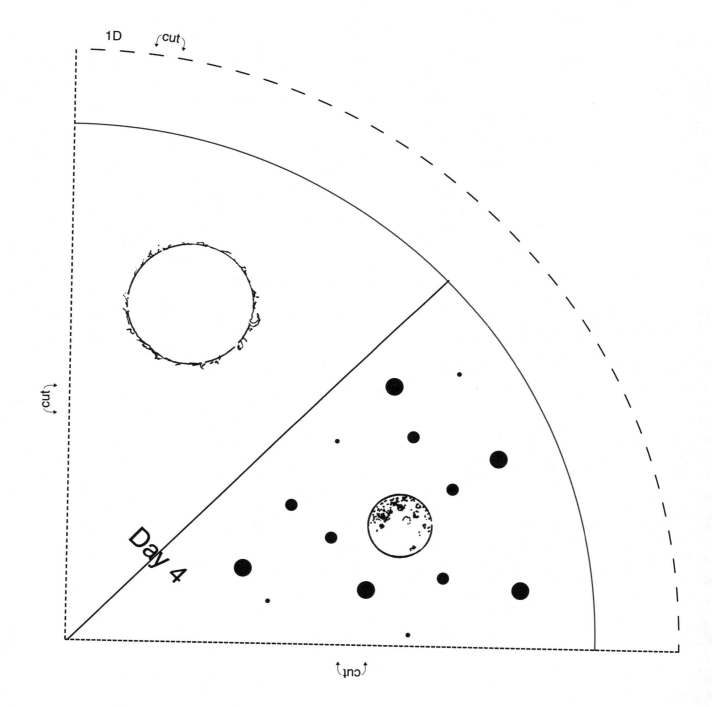

1D

cut

cut

Day 4

cut

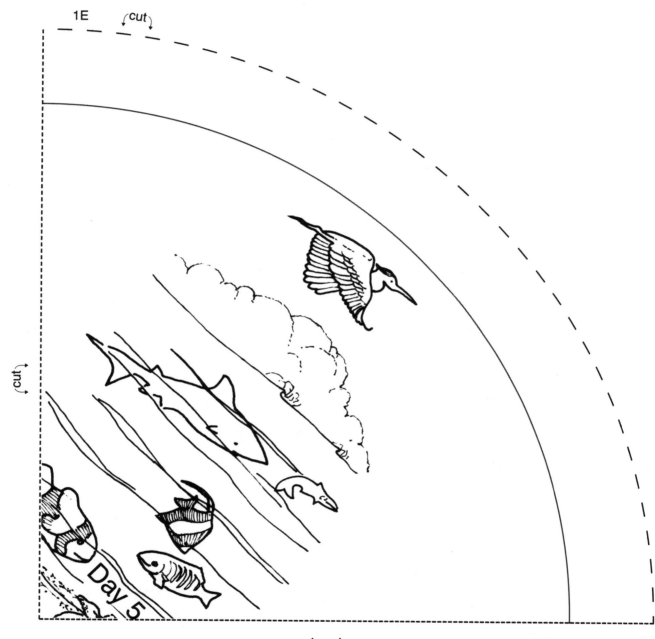

1E

cut

cut

cut

Day 5

1F

cut

cut

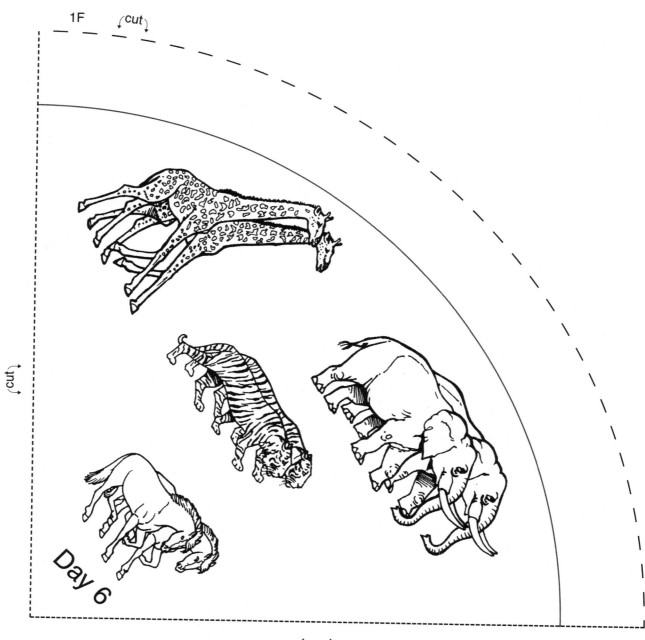

Day 6

cut

1G

cut

cut

cut

Day 6

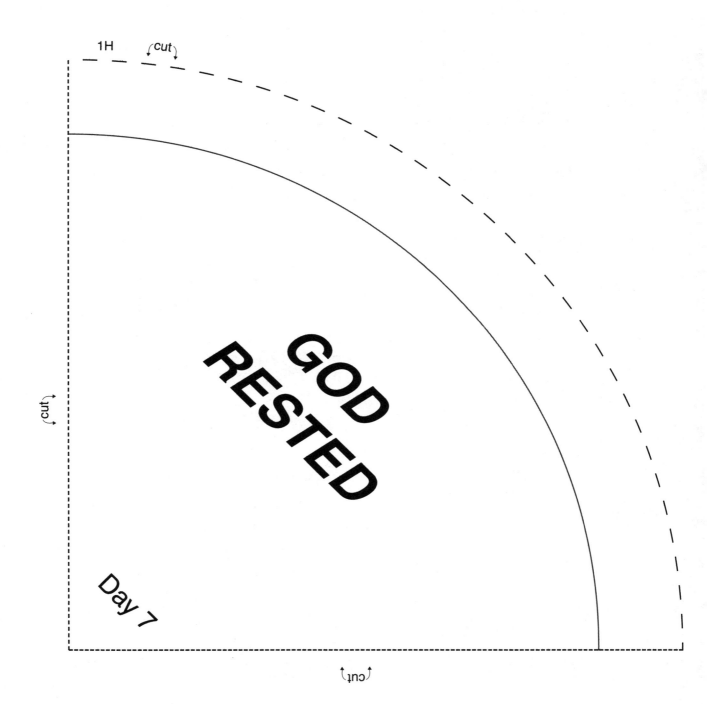

1H

cut

cut

GOD
RESTED

Day 7

cut

1I

1J

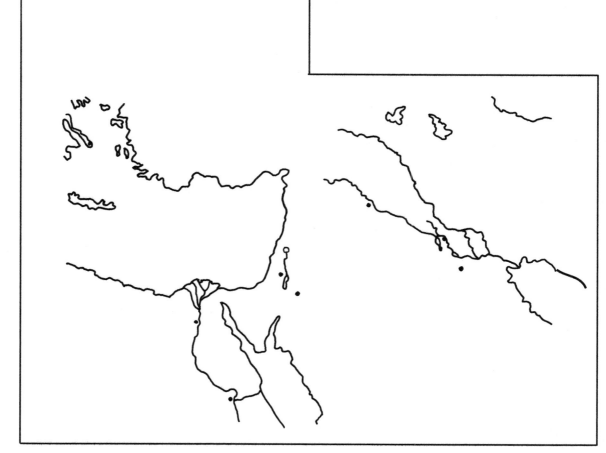

1K

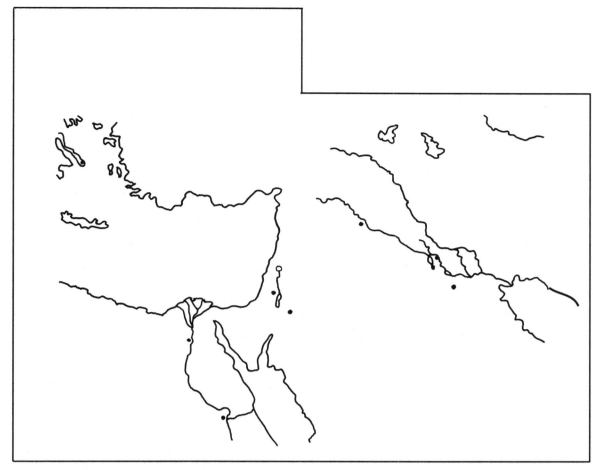

1L

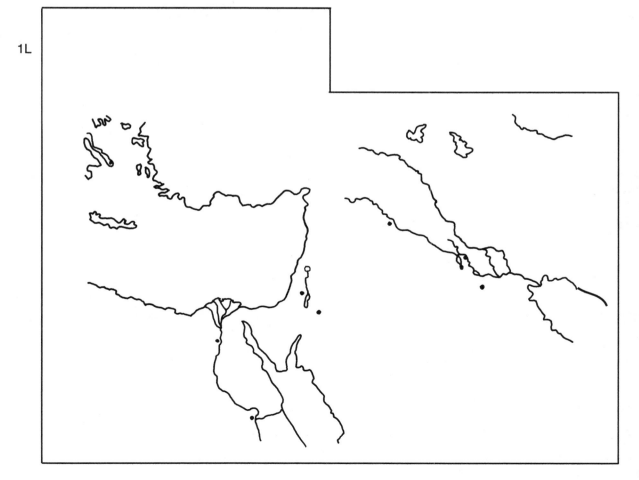

Pre-History

9000 B.C.

8001 B.C.

8000 B.C.

7001 B.C.

7000 B.C.

6001 B.C.

6000 B.C.

5001 B.C.

5000 B.C.

4001 B.C.

4000 B.C.

3001 B.C.

3000 B.C.

2001 B.C.

2000 B.C.

1001 B.C.

1000 B.C.

901 B.C.

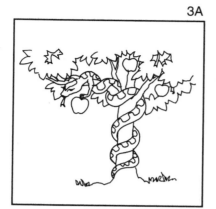

3A

3B

4A

4B

Timeline   4C

Timeline   4D

Timeline   4E

Timeline   4F

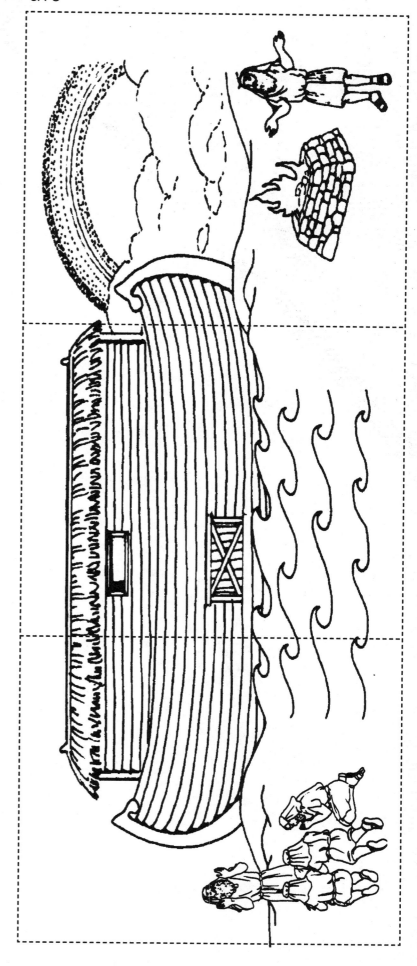

"**Noah found grace in the eyes of the Lord.**"

Genesis 6:18

5D

Timeline 5E

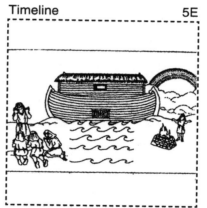

Timeline 5F

Timeline 5G

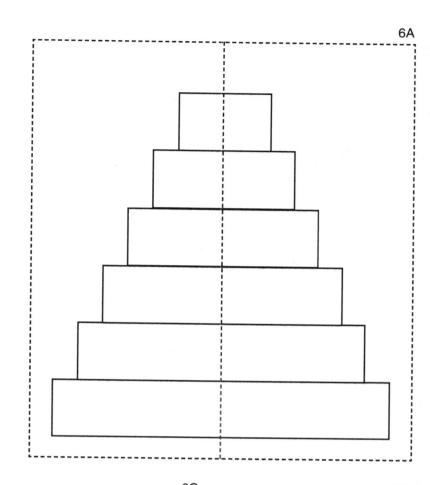

6A

6B

Visitor Pass

See the Pyramids

6C

Department of Immigration

Welcome to the Land of Moses

6D

Entry Permit

Jordan River

6E

Guest Pass

Ziggurat Tour

6F

Guest Pass

Caravan Express

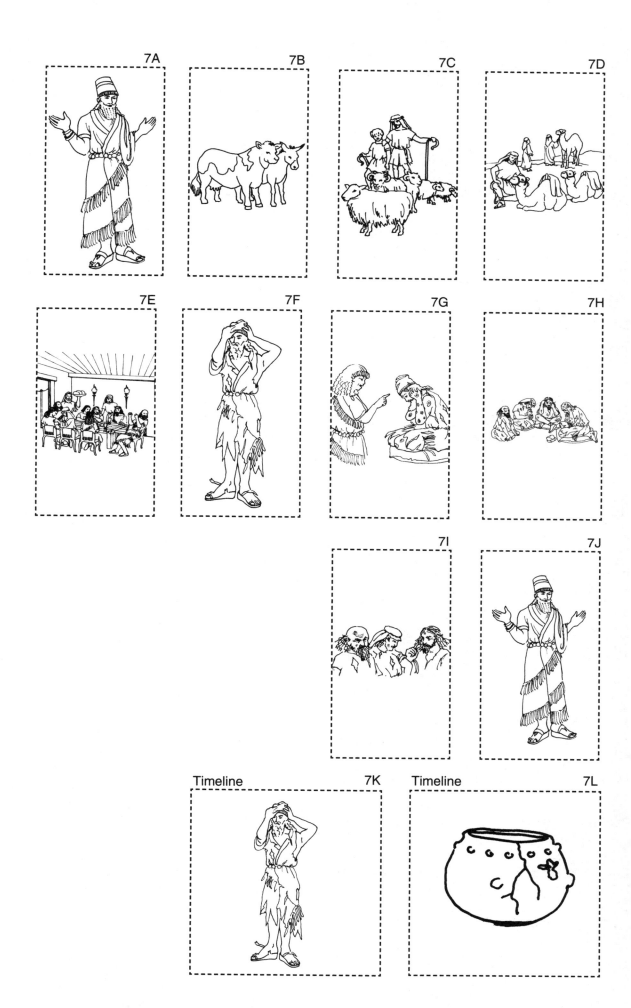

7A

7B

7C

7D

7E

7F

7G

7H

7I

7J

Timeline 7K

Timeline 7L

8A

Timeline 8B

Timeline 8C

Timeline 8D

Timeline 8E

9A

Timeline 9B

Timeline 9C

Timeline 9D

10A

Timeline

10B

11A

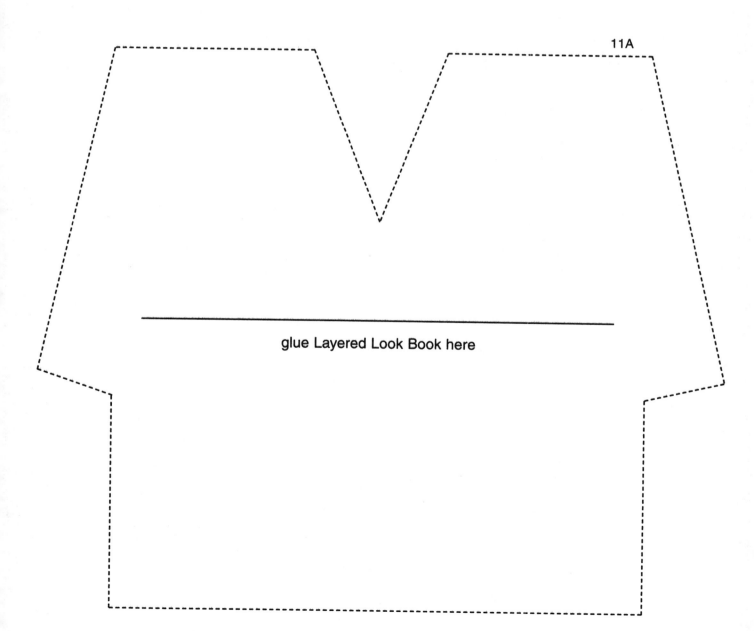

glue Layered Look Book here

11B

11C

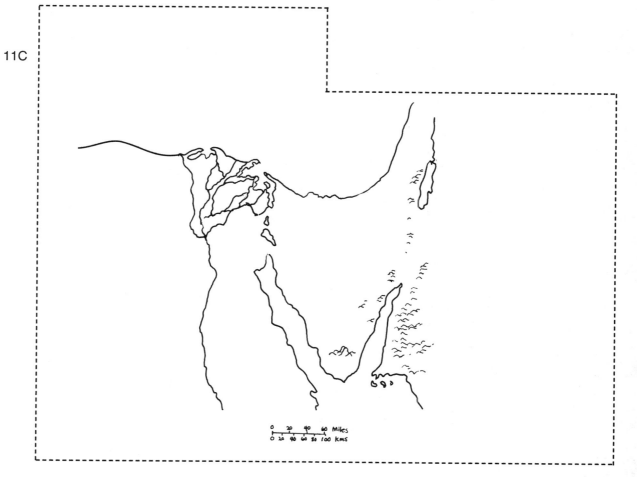

0   20   40   60 Miles
0 20 40 60 80 100 kms

11D

0   20   40   60 Miles
0 20 40 60 80 100 kms

11E

0   20   40   60 Miles
0 20 40 60 80 100 kms

0   20   40   60 Miles
0 20 40 60 80 100 kms

11F

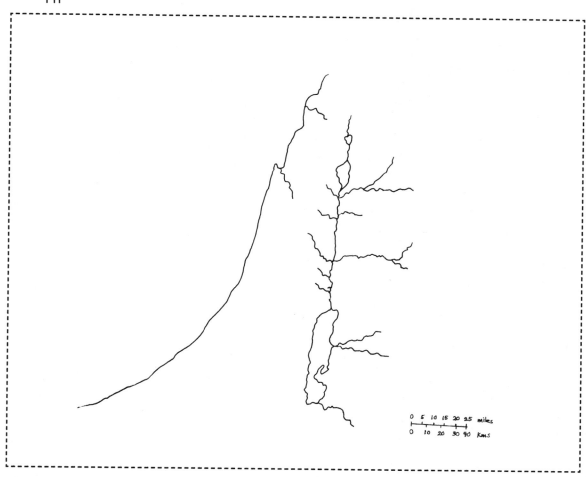

Timeline   11G

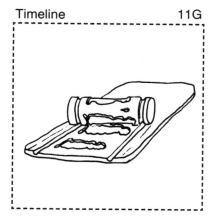

Timeline   11H

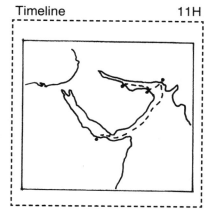

Timeline   11I

Timeline   12A

Timeline   12B

13A

13B

Timeline   13C

Timeline   13D

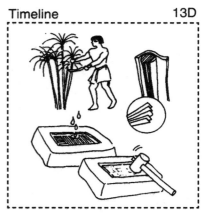

14A

14B

Timeline 14C

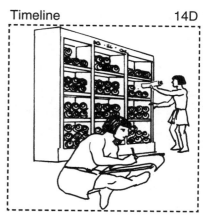

Timeline 14D

Moses

Pharaoh

blood

frogs

gnats

flies & insects

livestock diseases	boils	hail	locusts	darkness	death

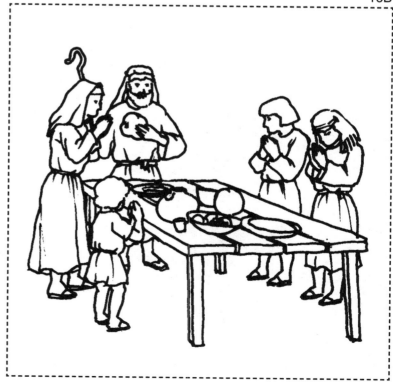

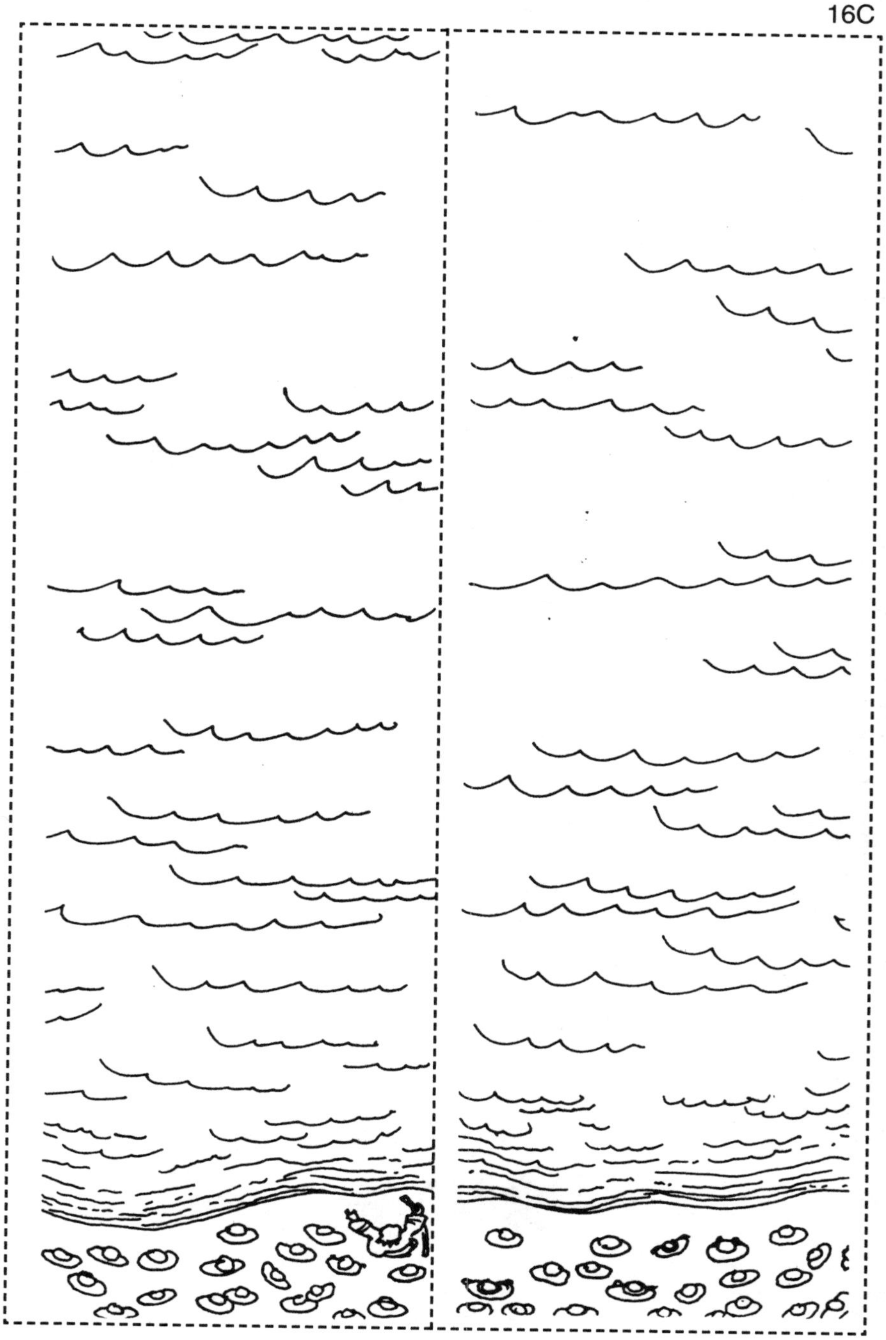

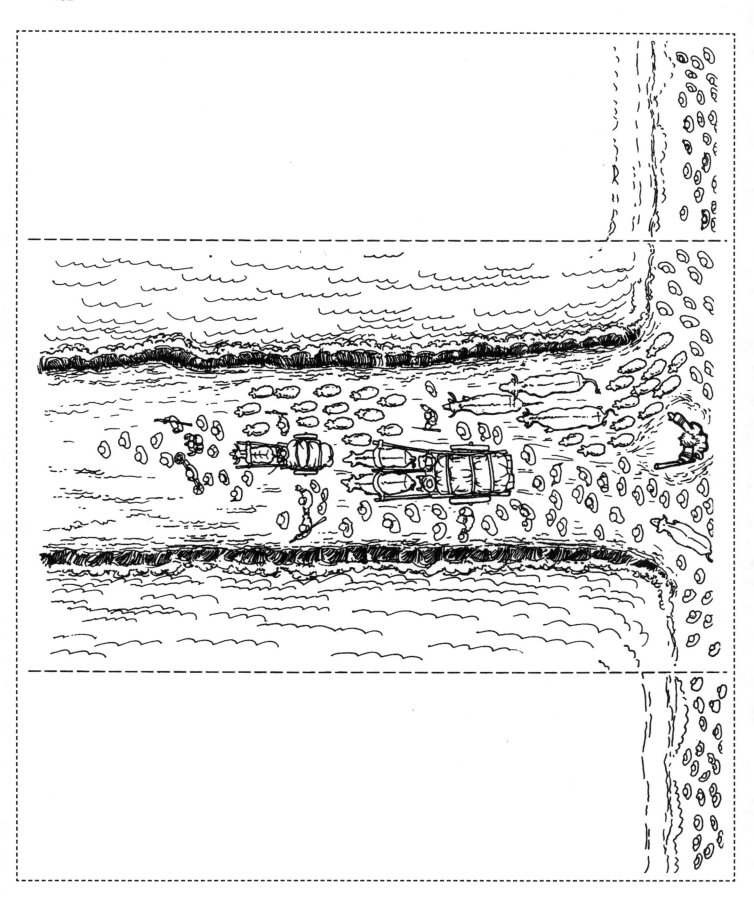

17A

17B

The Ten Commandments

 You shall not murder.

 You shall not commit adultery.

 You shall not steal.

 You shall not lie.

 You shall not covet your neighbor's house.

You shall have no other gods before Me.

 You shall not make for yourself a false idol or worship any other god but Me.

 You shall not take the name of the Lord in vain.

 Remember the sabbath day, to keep it holy.

 Honor your father and your mother.

Timeline 18B

Cattle

Bird

Wheat

Timeline 18C

19A-F

Tabernacle

Aaron

Artisans &
Metal Workers

Altar of
Burnt Offering

Laver

Altar of Incense

Lampstand	Table of Shewbread	Veil	Ark of the Covenant	Pillar of Cloud	Covering

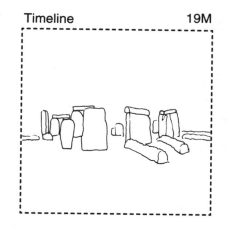

20A

20B

Timeline 20C

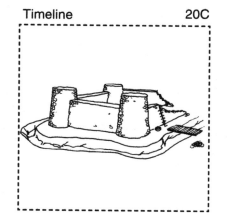

Timeline 20D

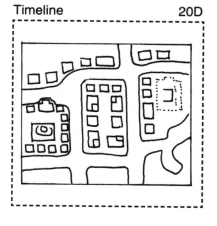

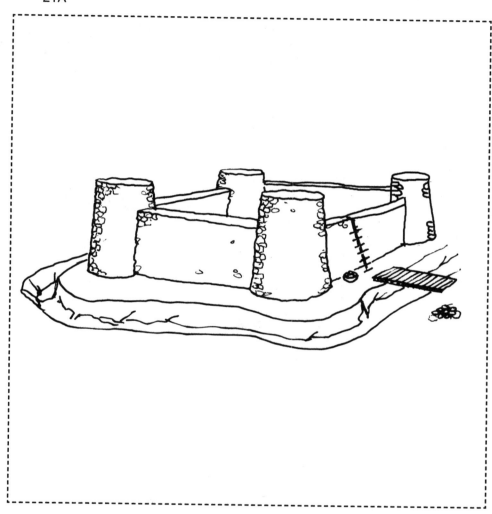

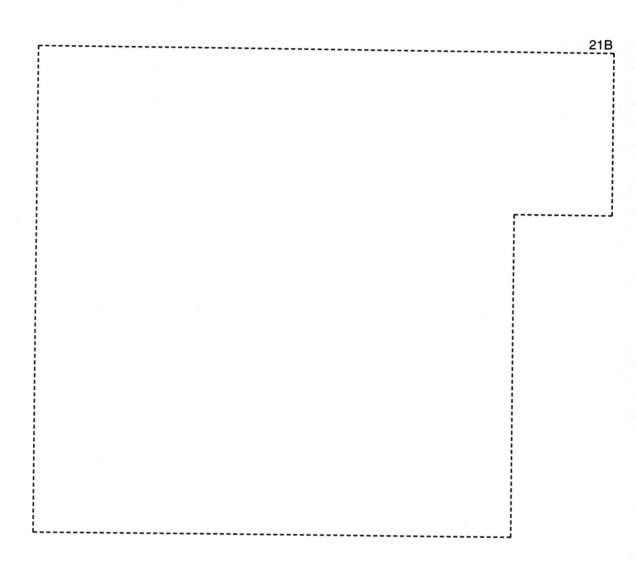

21B

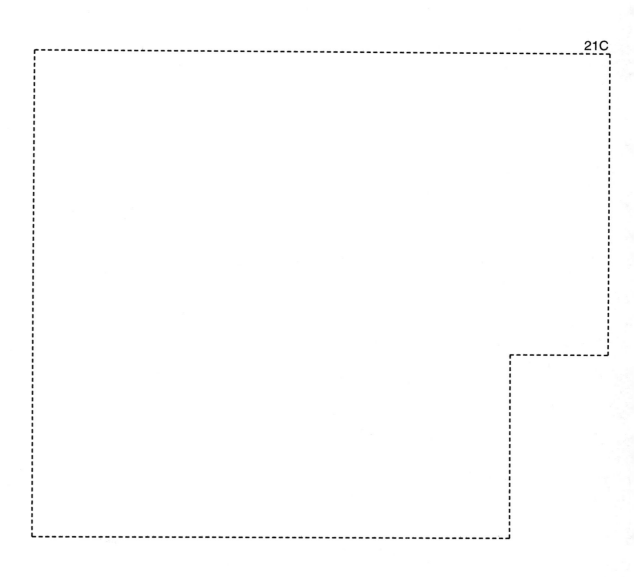

21C

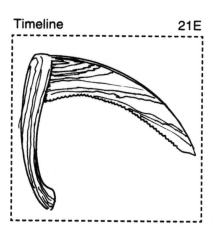

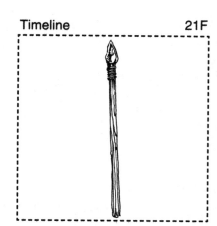

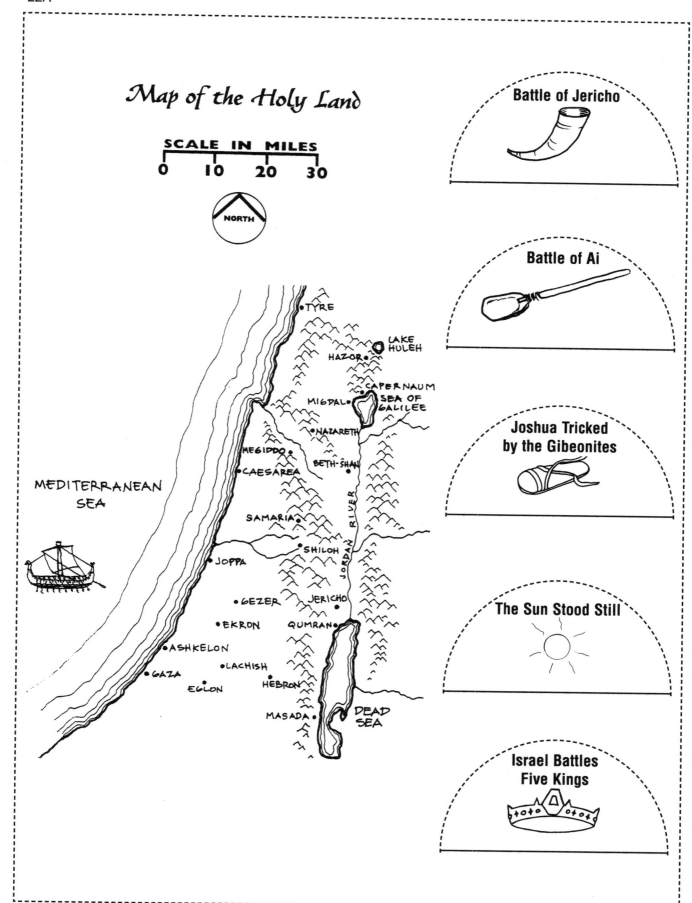

Map of the Holy Land

SCALE IN MILES

0   10   20   30

NORTH

TYRE

LAKE HULEH

HAZOR

CAPERNAUM

MIGDAL

SEA OF GALILEE

NAZARETH

MEGIDDO

BETH-SHAN

CAESAREA

MEDITERRANEAN SEA

SAMARIA

JORDAN RIVER

SHILOH

JOPPA

GEZER

JERICHO

EKRON

QUMRAN

ASHKELON

GAZA

LACHISH

EGLON

HEBRON

MASADA

DEAD SEA

Battle of Jericho

Battle of Ai

Joshua Tricked by the Gibeonites

The Sun Stood Still

Israel Battles Five Kings

Timeline 22B

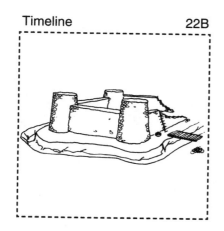

Timeline 22C

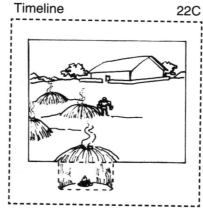

Timeline 22D

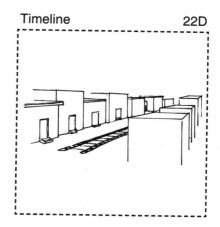

Timeline 23A

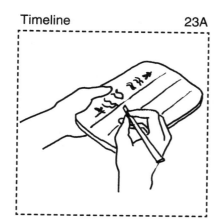

Timeline 23B

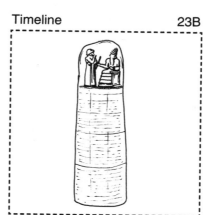

Timeline 23C

Timeline 24A

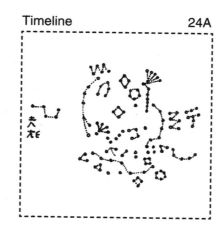

Timeline 24B